ROCKBOUND
ROCK'N'ROLL ENCOUNTERS

1955 TO **1969**

*For Michelle
Enjoy the memories*

Acknowledgments

How can you say thanks to everyone — or just about everyone — you have ever worked with? And especially all those who helped out during the research, writing, rewriting and editing of *Rockbound*. We cannot. So thanks to everyone who in some way helped us — you all know who you are.

Special thanks to Joanne Young and the kind staff at Vrlak/Robinson Advertising who gave up desks, typewriters and space with patience. Very special thanks to our spouses, Carole Robinson and John Hodgins, for their fortitude and their patience during the long haul. Hats off to Marilyn Loewen, Peggy Stewart, Dawn Stewart, Barbara Dobie, J. J. Richards, Tasia Richards, the late J. G. Keenan, Franne Gregg, Ben Kopelow, Eva Corrin, Ken Lundgren, Tom Peacock, Mel Cooper and Judy Brake, who helped us in so many ways.

We would also like to thank our mentors over the years, including the late "Tiny" Elphicke, Vic Waters, Al Jordan, Doug Greig, Don Hamilton, Allan Slaight, Jack Cullen, Jack Stewart, Hugh Pickett and Ivan Ackery. To our U.S. friends Gary Taylor, Bill Gavin, Dan Holliday, Don Porter and Chuck Blore, another vote of thanks. Finally, to Nancy Flight, our patient and understanding editor, a big thanks for helping us turn an elephantine amount of information into a semblance of order and, we hope, a darn good yarn.

Thanks also to Holiday Inns across Canada and the U.S.A. for the media and accomodation facilities they provided.

ROCKBOUND
ROCK'N'ROLL ENCOUNTERS

BY
RED ROBINSON
AND
PEGGY HODGINS

ISBN 0-88839-162-5
Copyright © 1983 Red Robinson & Peggy Hodgins

Catalog in Publication Data

Hodgins, Peggy & Robinson, Red
Rockbound rock 'n' roll encounters

ISBN 0-88839-162-5

1. Rock music — History and criticism. I. Hodgins, Peggy.
II. Title.
ML3534.R62   784.5'4'009   C82-091241-7

All rights reserved. No part of this publication may be reproduced, stored in a retrieval system, or transmitted, in any form or by any means, electronic, mechanical, photocopying, recording or otherwise, without the prior written permission of Hancock House Publishers.

"The Ordeal of Ringo's Ringer" on page 157 is reprinted with permission from Maclean's Magazine.

Edited by Nancy Flight
Typeset by Elizabeth Grant in Megaron
   on an AM Varityper Comp/Edit
Cover Design by Crystal Ryan
Layout Design by Eva Raidl
Production by Eva Raidl
Printed in Canada by Friesen Printers

Hancock House Publishers Ltd.
19313 Zero Ave., Surrey, B.C. Canada V3S 5J9

Table of Contents

Preface 6
Genesis of Rock 'n' Roll 8
1955 16
1956 26
1957 40
1958 72
1959 88
1960 102
1961 112
1962 124
1963 136
1964 154
1965 170
1966 184
1967 192
1968 200
1969 214
Dedication   Photo Credits 223
Glossary 224
Index 226

Preface

Why did we decide to write a book about rock'n'roll when there are so many books on the market already? We felt we had to set the record straight — if only to give a more positive view of how rock 'n' roll evolved and what the entertainers were really like. We feel many of these books contain mistakes or give an inaccurate impression of the era of rock 'n' roll. Most of the books feature the same stock photos and give the same general biographies of the rock 'n' roll stars — or, they go the other way and destroy our fond memories with gut-wrenching exposés.

As one of the pioneering deejays who first played rock 'n' roll and continued to play it over the next 16 years, Red was intimately involved in rock 'n' roll and had a unique vantage point. He was the gutsy teenager who introduced rock 'n' roll to radio listeners in British Columbia and subsequently influenced the Canadian music scene in broadcasting. He also met and interviewed such giants as Chuck Berry, Buddy Holly, Elvis Presley and Bill Haley and the Comets, as well as dozens — if not hundreds — of other stars. Besides his collection of interviews, Red had hundreds of photographs of the recording stars of the fifties and sixties. Red's involvement with rock 'n' roll from its beginning in the midfifties until 1969, his encounters with the stars and his unique collection of photographs all provided reasons for writing *Rockbound*.

Red had the raw material; now he needed someone who shared his interest in and knowledge of rock 'n' roll to help him turn this material into a book. That's where Peggy came in. She too had been an early rock 'n' roll fan, had participated in rock 'n' roll radio programs and had met Red during the days when West Coasters thought he was a star himself. Having worked in rock radio in Toronto and Vancouver and then continued a career of writing and broadcasting (which also included the research and writing of over 300 nostalgia radio shows), Peggy decided to write a book about her own experiences that had a more general perspective.

A chance luncheon with the two old pals in June 1981 resulted in the decision to make *Rockbound* a combined effort. After all, we had shared many of those moments in the late fifties and early sixties and had stayed in touch. We were about the same vintage, had read many of the same books and adored the halcyon days of early rock 'n' roll.

After months of assembling the material, we realized the book should be written from a first person point of view. Since Red consistently remained in radio since the fifties, had been an announcer and had met the majority of the stars, we decided the book would be written as his story. Some of the anecdotes are told from both of our recollections — making it even more interesting, we hope. In short: it is Red's story; it is Peggy's writing.

The word *rockbound* means "surrounded by rock." We chose that word for the title of the book because we felt that during the fifties and the sixties we *were* surrounded by rock. And it was firm, solid and, to quote a line from one of the songs, here to stay.

Some chapters of our book are richer in content than others. There is a reason for this difference. Some years were explosive — 1955, 1957 and 1964, for example. Others did not have that sizzle. These years saw the original rock 'n' roll explosion, the British invasion, the growth of flower power and the experimental rock become benchmarks in our story. Others were — yawn — years of stability and sometimes even boredom. But throughout all these phases, the rock 'n' roll era was a period unlike any other in modern history. It combined an entertainment revolution with a cultural revolution. Could it happen again? We doubt it. Programming of records is now done in such a businesslike manner a guy like Sam Cooke could not just ring the buzzer and ask that his record be played on a major-market radio station. But rock 'n' roll has been undergoing a renaissance which has been evident since 1980. And we think it will be around for a few more years.

This book is a salute to the artists and the entertainers, the backup guys, the composers, the ambitious agents, and, above all, the recording artists who made rock 'n' roll the historical musical contribution it became: Elvis Presley, Eddie Cochran, Buddy Holly, Ritchie Valens, Bill Haley, Gene Vincent, the Beatles, Pat Boone, Paul Anka, Diana Ross and all the rest. This book is our tribute to them.

Red Robinson
Peggy Hodgins

The Genesis of Rock'n'Roll

The Blacksmith Blues	**Ella Mae Morse**
The Blue Tango	**Leroy Anderson**
Botch-a-Me	**Rosemary Clooney**
Don't Let the Stars Get in Your Eyes	**Perry Como**
High Noon	**Frankie Laine**
I Went to Your Wedding	**Patti Page**
Jambalaya — on the Bayou	**Hank Williams**
Wheel of Fortune	**Kay Starr**
Your Cheatin' Heart	**Hank Williams**

Allez-Vous-En, Go Away	Kay Starr
Changing Partners	Patti Page
Ebb Tide	Frank Chacksfield
Gambler's Guitar	Frankie Laine
I Believe	Frankie Laine
Istanbul	The Four Lads
Rock around the Clock	Bill Haley and the Comets
Secret Love	Doris Day
Vaya con Dios	Les Paul and Mary Ford
You, You, You	The Ames Brothers

Little Things Mean a Lot	Kitty Kallen
Wanted	Perry Como
Hey There	Rosemary Clooney (Sammy Davis, Jr.)
Sh-Boom	The Crew Cuts
Make Love to Me	Jo Stafford
I Get So Lonely	Four Knights
Hernando's Hideaway	Archie Bleyer
Skokiaan	Ralph Marterie
Shake, Rattle and Roll	Bill Haley and the Comets

It's been more than 30 years since I first became involved in rock 'n' roll music. But it seems like yesterday. I still feel a shiver up and down my spine when I remember those first recordings I heard on American stations, which I could barely tune in on my radio in the East End of Vancouver.

Rock 'n' roll was never the "June, spoon" music that people had been used to. Maybe that's why adults cringed when they first heard it. Rock 'n' roll evolved from a variety of musical styles. It was an offshoot of jazz, blues, soul, and much more. It was as experimental in the late forties and early fifties as progressive jazz was.

To understand the genesis of rock 'n' roll, you have to study the music of the forties. These were the years of the Second World War, when dance bands, the Andrew Sisters and basically mediocre music were the fare of hit parades around the world.

Toward the end of the forties, black singers and entertainers began performing a new type of African jazz that had a strong, pulsating beat. It was a primitive style that also used the sounds of the old spirituals, which had been handed down from one generation to the next, beginning with the slaves. Much of this new music had its origins in New Orleans jazz, but it differed greatly from the traditional Dixieland, which is still popular today. Known as rhythm and blues, this new sound had more blues and more of a beat than the lyrical rhythmic jazz.

Before rock 'n' roll became an accepted music form, only a handful of record manufacturers dared to produce and release "race" records. Life was very black and white in those days. In the early days of rock, it was the small, independent record companies that bullied the equally small recording studios in North America into taking a chance on some of the "race" sounds. They produced what was known as specialized music — most of it "black" and much of it "country" in content.

Teams of enthusiastic, often hungry, and definitely ballsy promotion people hammered on the doors of small stations in order to gain radio exposure for their recording artists. Slowly a pattern emerged: small stations played the records, the records gained acceptance, and word eventually got around to the major markets. Soon larger stations with deejays who dared to be original began playing the records and letting more of the population know about them. I was one of the original eight bad-boy deejays who did just that.

Among those first labels to hit the "regular" airways after isolation on the predominantly black radio stations were King, Alladin, Jubilee, Atlantic, and Chess, to name just a few. I recall experimenting with those labels on my show at CJOR in Vancouver as early as 1953.

Because record playlists on radio stations throughout North America were racially segregated, it was almost impossible to program a combination of music by both black and white artists. Stations had very rigid personalities — they were white, black, country, easy-listening, or classical. Or, if they were affiliated with national networks, they aired everything from soap operas and news commentaries to plays, poetry, live music, and the latest records. The rhythm and blues charts published in many national magazines really referred to "Negro" music, which was aimed solely at the black audience through black radio stations. I remember after playing one of those records on the "white" radio station where I worked — just before rock 'n' roll took off — the phone rang and a voice snarled, "Nigger lover!"

In the early fifties, as black music began attracting beat-hungry white listeners, such white performers as the McGuire Sisters and Pat Boone began recording hits by black artists. "Shake, Rattle and Roll" was originally recorded by Joe Turner and then recorded for white listeners, or "covered," by Bill Haley and the Comets. "Sh-Boom" by the Chords became popular on the black stations and was instantly covered by the Crew Cuts for the white audience. Similarly, "Hearts of Stone" by the Charms showed up on the white charts by the very lyrical and definitely white Fontane Sisters.

Some of the pioneer deejays who played these records were Alan Freed in Cleveland, Dewey Phillips in Memphis, George "Hound Dog" Lorenz in Buffalo, Hunter Hancock in Los Angeles, and the young redhead, Red Robinson, in Vancouver. Alan Freed deserves a special mention in any history of rock 'n' roll. He was Mr. Rock 'n' Roll back in those days. From radio station WJW in Cleveland, Freed had developed a huge following that resulted in an unprecedented record sales. Realizing that much of his popularity was due to his innovative addition of rhythm and blues music, which he loved and which wasn't being played on other "white" radio stations — or other time slots on WJW — he began playing more and more rhythm and blues music until it dominated his show.

Alan Freed's theme was "Blues for Moon Dog" by Todd Rhodes on King Records. Throughout the song, Alan would bay like a dog howling at the moon. He stopped using the theme when a blind percussionist in New York who used the "Moon Dog" theme took legal action against Freed. Thereafter, Freed presented his "Rock 'n' Roll Party."

In 1954, Freed moved his program to WINS Radio in New York. He had begun writing music in 1949 when his "Tongue-Tied Blues" was recorded by blues artist Champion Jack Dupree. During the fifties, Alan wrote many of the hits recorded by the Moonglows. The most significant hit was a 1954 recording written with Harvey Fuqua called "Sincerely." Later, in June 1958, the Moonglows recorded "The Ten Commandments of Love." Freed came up with the group's name when he was at WJW doing the "Moondog Show."

Alan Freed was a pioneer in many ways. His attention to recordings, his diversity, and his personal charm made all of us see him as more than a peer. He was a deejay, a concert emcee, a booking agent, and, eventually, a movie producer. For reasons described later in this book, he did not end up a financial success. Regrettably, he died in Palm Springs, California, in 1965 with little fanfare. Shortly after his death, one of Freed's sons contacted me in Vancouver and asked me if I had any photos or information about his father. Apparently Freed never kept anything throughout his trailblazing career.

Freed was responsible for coining the phrase "rock 'n' roll." There are many anecdotes about how Freed happened to hit on the term." In 1966, Bill Haley told me that the phrase came from a line in an old blues lyric that goes, "My baby rocks me with a steady roll." Freed began using "rock 'n' roll" in preference to "rhythm and blues" because he felt there was a racial stigma to the latter.

Bill Haley had been a country western band leader and was the first to marry rhythm and blues and country music. Many radio programmers wouldn't touch his first releases, such as "Crazy Man, Crazy" — the first rock 'n' roll song to make *Billboard*'s national chart in 1953 — or "Rock Around the Clock," because they felt these songs were too much like rhythm and blues. Many radio station sales managers were afraid the station's advertisers might think the station was attracting a Negro clientele — the wrong type of demographics for a successful white radio station.

While black singers were singing the blues to the blacks, Hank Williams was singing the country blues about being poor to the white southerners. Both the poor whites and the blacks had some blues to sing about. When Memphis deejay Dewey Phillips — the first man in the world to play an Elvis record — began programming both rhythm and blues and country blues, the writing was on the wall — soon some smart record producer was going to find an artist that would combine the two. That's exactly what happened when Elvis Presley recorded his first songs on the small Sun label in Memphis. When Elvis blasted onto the scene, country and western blues added the final touches to rock 'n' roll, and its commercial acceptance was inaugurated.

Before rock 'n' roll became a music form to be taken seriously, the pop charts were dominated by 6 major recording companies. By 1952, there were over 100 independent companies in business. Most of them specialized in rhythm and blues or country music.

Fans of rhythm and blues — or rhythm 'n' blues, as the purist would call it — will recall such early numbers as "Open the Door, Richard," a 1947 hit featured in many vaudeville shows throughout North America. Louis Jordan was the blues singer who introduced that song, as well as "Caledonia," "Choo Choo Ch'Boogie," "Ain't Nobody Here But Us Chickens" (which made a comeback in the late seventies), "Reet, Petite and Gone," "Saturday Night Fish Fry," and "Blue Light Boogie." Born in 1908, Louis Jordan was a saxophonist, band leader, and songwriter. As late as 1964, he was signed by blues pianist Ray Charles to churn out hits for that musician's Tangerine label. Although the average fan on the street may not recognize his name, Jordan has had a great influence on the work of other singers. B. B. King continues to incorporate many Louis Jordan techniques into his shows and recordings, and Bill Haley readily acknowledged the influence of Louis Jordan on some of his arrangements.

By now, diehard rock 'n' roll fans are probably ready to scream, "What about Chuck Berry?" There isn't a rock 'n' roll musicologist in the world who wouldn't agree that Charles Edward Anderson Berry was one of the biggest forces in rock 'n' roll. We'll be referring to Chuck Berry over and over because he made such an important contribution to this musical genre. Bill Haley, Elvis Presley, the Beach Boys, the Beatles and the Rolling Stones all patterned many of their hits after the Chuck Berry formula. And here is a bit of trivia you may not know — the Beach Boys made their national debut on the charts in 1963 with "Surfin' U.S.A.," a surfing version of the Chuck Berry composition "Sweet Little Sixteen."

In 1955, Chuck Berry made a trip to Chicago that was to change his life. He auditioned for Chess Records by performing a song he had written called "Ida Red." It was a country music parody that nobody wanted to buy. When the Chess executives suggested he change the name, Chuck thought for a few minutes and, remembering the name of a cow from a third grade story, renamed the song "Maybelline." It went on to become one of the classics of rock 'n' roll music Fifties deejay and rock music guru Alan Freed was given credit for the upbeat tempo and the lyrics of the song.

Thus, from a handful of cities in the United States — Chicago, New York, Memphis, St. Louis, and New Orleans — came a whole new kind of music. Rock rolled across the continent and swiftly captured the imagination of the world — at least that portion of the world between the ages of 13 and 19.

Rock 'n' roll was the first teenage music ever produced. It was rebellious music. Rock 'n' roll blurred the distinction between classes — it didn't matter what you wore to school; it only mattered that you knew how to jive. This was the first example of the influence of mass media on teenagers. It was also the first time the expression "teenagers" became part of our everyday vocabulary.

Radio cross-fertilized country and rhythm and blues. Now when you heard "Louisana Man" by Rusty and Doug, a country blues hit, or "Mojo Man" by Lightnin' Hopkins, a rhythm and blues hit, the distinction didn't matter. It was all blues and it was a prelude to rock 'n' roll.

Rock 'n' roll was vulgar, common and original. It wasn't movie music — though it did make a splash in *Blackboard Jungle*. Nor was it Broadway or Tin Pan Alley. It was a teenage turn-on.

From rhythm and blues and rockabilly to rock 'n' roll, Chuck Berry, Carl Perkins, Bill Haley, Elvis Presley, Buddy Holly and a handful of others gave us a legacy that we'll never forget.

Top Ten Hits

1. **Cherry Pink and Apple Blossom White** — Perez Prado
2. **Rock around the Clock** — Bill Haley and the Comets
3. **Yellow Rose of Texas** — Mitch Miller
4. **Autumn Leaves** — Roger Miller
5. **Unchained Melody** — Les Baxter
6. **Davey Crockett** — Bill Hayes
7. **Love Is a Many Splendored Thing** — The Four Aces
8. **Sincerely** — The McGuire Sisters
9. **Ain't That a Shame** — Pat Boone
10. **Dance with Me, Henry** — Georgia Gibbs

On Broadway

The Diary of Anne Frank
Cat on a Hot Tin Roof
Damn Yankees
Will Success Spoil Rock Hunter?

On Television

Jack Benny
Dinah Shore
Johnny Carson
Lawrence Welk
Burns and Allen
Philadelphia Bandstand

Top Movies

Marty
Mister Roberts
Love Is a Many Splendored Thing
Picnic
Rose Tatoo

The Oscars

Best Picture	*Marty*
Best Director	*Delbert Mann* (Marty)
Best Actor	*Ernest Borgnine* (Marty)
Best Actress	Anna Magnani *(The Rose Tatoo)*
Best Supporting Actor	Jack Lemmon *(Mr. Roberts)*
Best Supporting Actress	Jo Van Fleet *(East of Eden)*
Best Song	*"Love Is a Many Splendored Thing"* by Sammy Fain and Paul Francis Webster from *Love Is a Many Splendored Thing*

Best Sellers

Auntie Mame
  Patrick Dennis

Bonjour Tristesse
  Francoise Sagan

Marjorie Morningstar
  Herman Wouk

Ten North Frederick
  John O'Hara

The Secret of Happiness
  Billy Graham

1955

By 1955, I belonged to a group of North American jive-talking deejays who enjoyed introducing new black artists to an audience. This group also included George "Hound Dog" Lorenz of Buffalo and Al Jarvis of Los Angeles, who are no longer around to relate these stories. There were a few others also. Although we are now considered the forerunners of the Top 40 era, we were considered the "bad boys" then, simply because we played rock 'n' roll and rhythm and blues.

In 1955, the U.S. Supreme Court gave local authorities throughout the United States the task of integrating schools. Concurrent with this historic event was the emergence of black music. Despite the racial problems in North America at the time, white kids appreciated black music and wanted to know more about it.

One of the groups we really enjoyed was the Platters. They were managed by Buck Ram, who had previously managed a group called the Penguins. The Platters were terrific. They had begun on the smaller King label in Los Angeles in 1953. By 1955, they had released "Only You," which was on the charts for 22 weeks in succession. From then until 1960, their very professional act, and especially the smooth vocals of tenor Tony Williams, assured them a spot in the Top 20 just about every year.

Other performers we responded to were singing about "Black Denim Trousers and Motor Cycle Boots" — a song actually recorded by the Cheers on Capitol Records. Many radio stations refused to play this song because they felt it was contributing to juvenile delinquency.

To the adult world, some of the lyrics continued to be scandalous. In addition to "Money Honey" and "Honey Love," the Drifters had a song called "Make Me Feel Real Loose, like a Long Neck Goose," which many nonfollowers of rock 'n' roll found offensive. "Oh, baby, that's what I like," a line out of a song by the Big Bopper also offended this group. By now, the term "rock 'n' roll" was almost an expletive to those who didn't care for the music. Considering some of the songs from the sixties, seventies and eighties — "Satisfaction" by the Rolling Stones, for example — it seems amusing that rock 'n' roll was offensive to so many people in the fifties.

1955

Rock 'n' roll was not the only phenomenon making waves in the fifties. Television was having just as much of an impact. Now, instead of going to the movies, families could sit around in their living rooms and enjoy the same kind of entertainment. Movie theaters were almost empty as people clustered around their little black and white screens at home.

Despite the sorry state of movies in general, two movies that came out in 1955 had an enormous effect on teenagers. One was *The Blackboard Jungle*. This brutally realistic movie was one of the first to show teenagers in a state of turmoil. In addition, the producer had heard "Rock around the Clock" by Bill Haley and the Comets and asked Haley to perform the song in the film. It was an instant hit and to this day remains synonymous with *The Blackboard Jungle*.

The other movie was *Rebel without a Cause*, which starred James Dean as a sensitive adolescent fighting the world of conformity. The film catapulted Dean to stardom, but, tragically, he was killed at dusk on September 30, 1955, in California, driving his Porsche Spyder. Ironically, he had just completed a short film on the merits of safe driving.

From that point on, my generation made the ghost of James Dean the focus of our rebellion against the norm and adult values. To us, James Dean was the symbol of that midfifties lost generation so aptly described by writer Jack Kerouac as the beat generation.

Down in Nashville in 1955, a former truck driver, Elvis Presley, was named outstanding new country artist of the year. He had been recording on the Sun label at the time, and in 1955 he signed he now-famous recording contract with RCA. Many thought Presley sounded like a black singer — just as many had thought that Buddy Holly must have been black to have so much "rhythmic ability."

James Dean and Elvis Presley belong together in this book because when Elvis Presley burst into the limelight he was like a reincarnation of James Dean. Maybe that was part of his power.

Another star who fell into the James Dean category was Marlon Brando, his motorbike paralleling Elvis Presley's guitar. Both Brando and Presley had dark hair, sideburns and an indefinable charisma that attracted millions of followers — then and now.

1955

Like James Dean, Elvis Presley was a "lost boy" we could identify with. In addition, Presley was the catalyst for rock 'n' roll, tying it all together with Bill Haley and Chuck Berry, who first ignited the fuse of rock 'n' roll.

All of a sudden, those of us who were teenagers began to have a voice. As we became aware of the changes in our bodies and of the opposite sex, we also discovered a new kind of music and developed a new set of values. Through rock 'n' roll, we saw ourselves the way we were — not as others saw us. It was a time of change, an exciting time to be alive and growing up. Almost every day, a new record was released, a new fad in clothes emerged, and there was something new and exciting for teenagers in North America to talk about.

For the first time in history, teenagers had economic power. We all seemed to be resourceful — pumping gas, working as soda jerks, cleaning, babysitting, or doing odd jobs after school. As we flocked to the record stores with our spending money, the average age of the record buyer began to plummet. The majority of buyers had previously been young adults in their twenties, but by 1958 teenagers were buying 75 per cent of all the records sold in North America. These statistics probably held true in the British Isles and Europe as well.

While adults were staying home to watch TV, we were going to the movies. Every Saturday afternoon we lined up to see the movie — often a double-feature — no matter who was playing. We might try to catch an early evening movie during the week as well. Going to the movies was a big occasion; romances began as young people paired off after they had bought their tickets! (The big test, of course, was when the fellow took his steady date and paid for her ticket.) If you're over the age of 35, you'll know what I mean when I say the last three rows of the movie theaters were the most popular. The back row was *THE* spot to be in. The record and movie companies were forced to recognize that this younger generation had money. To survive, they had to cater to the whims and wishes of teenagers.

For the first time, teenagers were buying cars. Hot rods raced down side streets and, unfortunately, many young hot rodders imitated the movies by playing "chicken" on the highway, leading to numerous accidents and deaths. That's how drag strips came about — for safety.

1955

The custom car people were not draggers. They tore apart old cars and covered them with coat after coat of shellac. Then they polished them and put in such innovations as carpeting on the floor and vinyl and ended up redesigning the car altogether.

As a result, teenagers influenced the style of new cars. Detroit took note of all this amateur activity and started making changes to attract further business from teenagers. It was the teenager of the fifties who put new tires on cars. A lot of what we take for granted in automobiles today — carpeting, the basic design and lines, stripes around the side — came about during this era. Car accessory companies and other custom facilities are also the legacy of those enterprising teenagers of the fifties.

As a disc jockey, I knew that you had to retain your popularity and build up your ratings. For this reason, I used to cover drag racing on my own time. This was in addition to the long hours I worked each week at the radio station — split shifts and 12-hour days were just part of the long, 7-day weeks we all put in.

I used to go out to the Abbotsford Airport near Vancouver, B.C., where the world-famous Abbotsford Air Show is now held yearly and where drag racing used to be held. I would do interviews, cover the events, talk to the winners and tape the sound of the cars screaming down the strip. Sometimes I would climb into the car with the driver and make a tape as we whirled and screeched down the raceway. Then I'd take the tape back and play it on the air so my listeners could experience the excitement of the drag race.

I used to do my CJOR afternoon radio show at the old playhouse on Howe Street, where Robson Square stands today. I would play those fabulous old rhythm and blues songs and the kids in the audience would suddenly jump up and start dancing in the aisles — they just couldn't sit still. This was something unusual. Frank Sinatra had the older women swooning, but he didn't have the kids dancing in the aisles.

By 1955, after only a few years on the air, my CJOR afternoon show was heard by 53 per cent of the British Columbia and Northwest Washington radio audience. This was happening in every major city in North America — the rock 'n' roll stations were getting the ratings. The new sound and the "shook up" generation was taking over.

1955

Like many adults, a few of my peers at CJOR and the heads of other stations across North America, the CJOR management didn't like the music at all. But a cardinal rule of management in any business is: if it brings in revenue, it stays.

My first sponsor was 7-Up, which bought an hour's worth of air time five days a week for a year. This was unheard of in Vancouver at the time. So when the radio station sales manager saw the contract and realized that the appeal of other types of radio shows was dwindling, he took note. Radio was definitely changing direction.

At this time, most radio stations were employing announcers with big voices. These guys were definitely not disc jockeys. They introduced the records very formally and authoritatively, and their programs had an impersonal structure. This was particularly true in Canada, where the star announcer was Lorne Greene. After a stint at CBC, he started his own announcers' school to train other formal announcers. Greene wisely graduated to voicing commercials (which he still does today) and then began acting on television, where he made "Bonanza" his rightful home. Can you imagine Lorne Greene be-bopping, jiving and introducing "Don't Be Cruel"?

Along with other "maverick" deejays, I had a real free-form program going where I'd talk to the kids on the phone and send out dedications, pull pranks and ad-lib constantly. Ad-libbing at that time simply wasn't done. Normally the "continuity" department of a radio station developed scripts for the announcers, or else they would do nothing more than announce the title of the record they were about to play. Think of a staid FM station — there's one in just about every major North American market — and you've got the mood of an old-time fifties AM radio sound stuck in the "Maple Leaf Ballroom" syndrome. No wonder radio was in trouble.

Don't blame the announcer. Those were his orders. If he was going to do a show on Glenn Miller, Glen Gray, or Tommy Dorsey, he was restricted to just that. He was not supposed to use teenage lingo or refer to any of the latest fads. As a result, he wasn't with it, cool, or "real George," as we used to say.

The old-fashioned radio announcers weren't the only casualties of the rock 'n' roll wave. Before 1955, various musical shows, including "Your Hit Parade" out of New York and "Cross-

1955

Canada Hit Parade" out of Toronto, were popular among teenagers. After 1955, however, these shows faded from the scene — Dorothy Collins of "Your Hit Parade" couldn't get into "You Ain't Nothing But a Hound Dog." By 1957, these shows had disappeared forever.

Singers Vic Damone and Doris Day were two others who never recovered from the blow of rock 'n' roll, although they had made the general charts before 1955 with a battery of hits. Can you imagine Doris Day singing "Shake, Rattle and Roll"? Nevertheless, with the help of her manager, Doris Day was able to make a glut of comedy girl-next-door movies with James Garner, Cary Grant, Rock Hudson and Tony Randall. One of her few musical success after 1955 was "Que Sera, Sera," or "Whatever Will Be, Will Be," written by Jay Livingston and Ray Evans, which she sang in the movie *The Man Who Knew Too Much* and for which she won an Oscar in 1956.

This changing record, music, movie and radio world also threatened to hurl such recording stars as Rosemary Clooney, Perry Como and Jo Stafford into obscurity. Clooney and Como would resurface on television, but for Jo Stafford there would be no more glorious tomorrows.

Who were the other first ladies of entertainment when rock hit the scene? Patti Page, whose hit "Tennessee Waltz" was standard fare in dimly lit gymnasiums during proms; Teresa Brewer, who belted out "Music, Music, Music"; and Peggy Lee, whose novelty Mexican tune "Manana" took off like lightning. Peggy Lee later thrilled North American deejays in person at the infamous Miami Disc Jockey Convention in 1958 and continued a successful career as a ballad, blues and jazz singer. She remains one of my all-time favorites. Others were not so talented or flexible and did not survive the changing times.

Despite the huge impact of rock 'n' roll, it would be misleading to suggest that rock 'n' roll was everything in 1955. It wasn't. In the early fifties, one of the most successful recording artists was Harry Belafonte, whose RCA album *Calypso* was the first LP to sell 1,000,000 copies. The Calypso craze was encouraged by adults, and suddenly everything was calypso, from music to food, clothes and travel. Although the calypso craze didn't last, Harry Belafonte did, branching out into folk music, ballads, and acting. Today he remains

1955

a superstar in the entertainment industry, though to the youth of the seventies and eighties he is probably better known as a film and TV star than a recording artist.

Frank Sinatra had a hit with "Love and Marriage," and Jackie Gleason's *Lonesome Echo*, *Romantic Jazz*, *Music, Martinis and Memories* and *Music for Lovers Only* were among the top five albums of the year. Other non-rock 'n' roll hits of the year were "Yellow Rose of Texas" by Mitch Miller, "Autumn Leaves" by Roger Williams, and "Moments to Remember" by Canada's Four Lads.

Nineteen fifty-five was also the year for slumber parties, shoe taps and strapless prom dresses with frothy nylon tulle — you couldn't get near the girl you were dancing with. Then there were cinch belts, strange-colored lipstick, Bermuda shorts, cropped hair and sequins.

For me, 1955 was the year I attended dozens of sock hops, met thousands of teenagers with similar aspirations and enjoyed living to the hilt every day.

But most important, in 1955 we saw the transition from pop — often called "silly pop" as performed by Eddie Fisher, Frankie Laine and Perry Como — to rhythm and blues and rock 'n' roll. Alarmed by this change, *Billboard* magazine ran an ad cautioning "adults and others" — meaning people in the music business, and especially record stores and jukebox operators — to "Keep pop alive in '55." Adults, which of course meant parents, were calling the new music a "teenage fad" and assumed that, like puppy love, it would quickly fade away. It didn't.

CJOR studios, Vancouver, 1955.

A group of Vancouver cheerleaders joins me in the CJOR studio, 1955.

Top Ten Hits

1. Heartbreak Hotel — Elvis Presley
2. Don't Be Cruel — Elvis Presley
3. Lisbon Antigua — Nelson Riddle
4. My Prayer — The Platters
5. Wayward Wind — Gogi Grant
6. Hound Dog — Elvis Presley
7. Poor People of Paris — Les Baxter
8. Whatever Will Be, Will Be (Que Sera, Sera) — Doris Day
9. Memories Are Made of This — Dean Martin
10. Rock and Roll Waltz — Kay Starr

On Broadway

Auntie Mame
My Fair Lady
Mr. Wonderful
The Most Happy Fella
Li'l Abner
Bells Are Ringing
Long Day's Journey into Night

On Television

Kraft Theatre
$64,000 Question
Father Knows Best
Amos 'n' Andy
Talent Scouts

Top Movies

Around the World in 80 Days
Friendly Persuasion
Giant
The King and I
The Ten Commandments

The Oscars

Best Picture	*Around the World in 80 Days*
Best Director	George Stevens *(Giant)*
Best Actor	Yul Brynner *(The King and I)*
Best Actress	Ingrid Bergman *(Anastasia)*
Best Supporting Actor	Anthony Quinn *(Lust for Life)*
Best Supporting Actress	Dorothy Malone *(Written on the Wind)*
Best Song	"Whatever Will Be, Will Be" *(Que Sera, Sera)* by Jay Livingston and Ray Evans from *The Man Who Knew Too Much*

Best Sellers

A Certain Smile
  Francoise Sagon

Peyton Place
  Grace Metallious

Profiles in Courage
  John F. Kennedy

The Search for Bridey Murphy
  Morey Bernstein

Don't Go Near the Water
  William Brinkley

1956

By 1956, rock 'n' roll was solidly entrenched in the Top 50 across North America and in other parts of the world where pop music was played.

Elvis Presley not only had three hits in the Top 10, but also held the number 14 spot with "I Want You, I Need You, I Love You." In addition, songs that he had cut on the old Sun label were big in the southern United States.

Mixed in with the rock 'n' roll sound was a variety of hits, including "Canadian Sunset," made popular by Eddie Heywood and Hugo Winterhalter; "Green Door," which disc jockey Jim Lowe wrote and recorded and which was terrific for jiving; "Blue Suede Shoes" by Carl Perkins, whose roots were rockabilly; and "Blueberry Hill" by Fats Domino.

When Gene Vincent's recording of "Be-Bop-A-Lula" came out, it is reported that Elvis Presley's mother said to him, "I like your new recording." Elvis answered, "But it isn't mine!" The age of impersonators was upon us; everyone wanted to cash in on the success of Elvis Presley. Over 20 years later, after his death, a new generation of impersonators would try to cash in on the Presley myth.

Remember "Why Do Fools Fall in Love?" with Frankie Lymon and the Teenagers? "Long Tall Sally" by Little Richard was popular, and you can't forget Bill Haley and the Comets' recording of "See You Later, Alligator," which became a catchword for everyone from toddlers to teenagers and their parents. A hint of things to come from overseas was the skiffle music from England made popular by Lonnie Donegan, who recorded "Rock Island Line" and had all the would-be folk singers humming along.

Through radio and television, we were able to witness an entirely new phenomenon in entertainment. The impact of hearing black performers on the radio and seeing them on TV was amazing for the time. Now it was out in the open. You could hear Sarah Vaughan, Ella Fitzgerald, B.B. King, and many others in restaurants on the occasional jukebox — and you could buy their records in the stores without having to mumble your request.

Back in 1956, I had heard people say, "Oh, it's just rock 'n' roll music I hate." This was a subtle form of bigotry. What they were really saying was, "I don't like my children dancing to, listening to, or buying

1956

negro records." But while the black singers continued to be referred to as "rhythm and blues" artists, they were slowly becoming part of rock 'n' roll, as their records were played on "white" radio stations.

In 1956 Irvin Feld — who now owns Ringling Bros. Barnum & Bailey — brought the "Show of Stars" to the old Georgia Auditorium in Vancouver. The lineup included Bill Doggett, the Five Satins, Fats Domino, Chuck Berry, Frankie Lymon and the Teenagers, Eddie Cooley, Laverne Baker and Clyde McPhatter.

I emceed the show and had the privilege of meeting and interviewing each of the stars. Chuck Berry's original songs and extraordinary guitar playing made him particularly impressive. Over the years he has been copied by many rock 'n' roll groups, including the Beach Boys, the Beatles and the Rolling Stones.

Chuck's first big hit was "Maybelline," which he wrote with Russ Frato and Alan Freed and recorded to great success in 1955. Over the next 17 years he had a string of hits that included "No Money Down," "Roll Over Beethoven," "School Days," "Thirty Days," "Sweet Little Sixteen" and "My Little Ding-a-Ling," which became a best seller in 1972.

Most of the stars who appeared at the 1956 "Show of Stars" presentation were listed in the rhythm and blues sections of the trade publications. Rock 'n' roll would change that later, but in 1956 these were the rhythm and blues hits and hitmakers.

When Bill Doggett introduced "Honky Tonk" to the world, he brought a classic instrumental that became one of the most danceable tunes of all time. Bill was no amateur and he gave a lot of respectability to the new music we were hearing. He had arranged music for Lionel Hampton, Louis Jordan, Count Basie and Louis Armstrong, and he had played backup piano for the Ink Spots. Bill put his combo together in 1952 and began recording for King Records.

Clyde McPhatter had formed a new singing group in 1953 with entertainers who had come out of other groups and drifted together — which is why they called themselves the Drifters. Their first hit together was a Jesse Stone classic called "Money Honey." Among the many well-known entertainers who passed through the Drifters over the years were Bobby Hendricks and Ben E. King.

Through the "Show of Stars" I gained a real understanding of

I enjoyed Fats Domino, shown here in 1956. His recording of "My Blue Heaven" is a classic.

"My fame won't last," Bill Haley told me in 1956, but "there's a kid named Elvis in Memphis who really has it."

Typical dance scenes from 1956 sock hops.

1956

the roots of rock 'n' roll. I had always appreciated Bill Haley and Elvis Presley, but after this amazing show in Vancouver I understood where it had all begun.

The credit for rock 'n' roll belongs unquestionably, to the American negroes, as they were referred to at that time. The blacks had given us jazz, and now they were spinning out another offering that would take the world by storm.

Guy Mitchell has always been one of my favorite stars — mainly because my first big show with a well-known artist was with this popular recording star of the fifties and sixties. In Vancouver, he appeared at the Sunset Community Centre, which has been tagged the "house that Bing built." Bing Crosby officially opened the place and it features a full-wall photographic blowup of Bing atop a bulldozer plowing up dirt for the building.

I was broadcasting my show "Theme for Teens" live from Sunset for that week and Guy had been invited to join me. We played records and Guy talked to the teenagers, autographed pictures and generally made the show an event.

In 1956, the crew cut was in. When the Canadaires were introduced to Cleveland deejay Bill Randle, he took one look at them and suggested they change their name to the Crew Cuts. They did and — not necessarily because of the name change or hairstyle — went on to record one of the pioneer rock hits of all time. "Sh-Boom" had been a rhythm and blues hit for the Chords, a black group. Naturally, a white cover record was required for those stations that didn't play black music, and the wonderfully harmonious ability of Rudi Maugeri, Pat Barrett, Ray Perkins and John Perkins made the Crew Cuts' version a more than respectable "cover" record.

Nineteen fifty-six was also the year that Elvis Presley's first motion picture, *Love Me Tender*, was released and shown at the Capitol Theatre in downtown Vancouver. Advance promotion for this movie was incredible. Vancouver has had a reputation for innovative movie merchandising for decades. Ivan Ackery, the wizard who operated and directed the Orpheum Theatre in Vancouver, has his own book out on the subject. Many entertainers throughout the world remember Ivan for his enthusiasm, his love of movies, and his success in hauling in the moviegoers even if the movie turned out to be a dud.

1956

In this case, the Capitol outdid itself — and probably, for once, outdid my old pal Ivan Ackery — with a publicity campaign that people still talk about.

When I arrived back in the city after a Vancouver Island sock hop, I was amazed. I was rushing to the theatre to go on stage and introduce the movie, and I couldn't get near the place! Blocks and blocks of teenagers — I thought it must be every teenager in the city — had lined up and were waiting to get in to see *Love Me Tender*.

Any movie critic will tell you that *Love Me Tender* was quite an ordinary movie. But when Elvis made his appearance on the screen, the girls screamed with delight in an unabashed show of emotion and sexuality. History would repeat itself with the Beatles and other groups, but Elvis was the first to get this kind of response.

As people were coming out of the theatre, I asked them their impression of the movie. Of the ten people I queried, only one woman was able to tell me anything at all about the story line of *Love Me Tender*. Elvis was the only reason that anyone went to the movie. Even the guys were more interested in how he sang and how he acted than what happened in the movie.

Elvis had an unprecedented number of hits at the top of the playlist in 1956. During that year, an estimated 90 million records were sold, topping the previous high of 80 million the year before. Of these 90 million records, 10 million were by Elvis Presley.

Even before *Love Me Tender* was released as an album, RCA had received nearly one million orders for it. The half-million dollars that Elvis earned from record sales in 1956 was only a portion of his earnings that year. (Translate that amount into 1983 dollars, and you realize what a whopping sum that was.)

School teacher Mae Axton wrote Elvis's first song, "Heartbreak Hotel." If Mae's last name sounds familiar, it's because her son, Hoyt Axton, became one of the most prolific songwriters of the sixties and seventies. Two of his hit songs in the early seventies were "Joy to the World" and "Never Been to Spain," both written for Three Dog Night. Hoyt also wrote "Greenback Dollar" for the Kingston Trio.

In 1956, Canadian broadcaster Jack Cullen booked Bill Haley and the Comets into the Kerrisdale Arena in Vancouver and asked me to help him emcee the show. I started my introduction and

Bill Doggett became one of the few musicians to bridge rock 'n' roll and jazz. Vancouver, 1956.

Barbara Ann Davie won a date with Robert Wagner during a CJOR promotion in 1956.

My friend Guy Mitchell with me and some "Theme for Teen" fans trying out for the cheerleading spot, 1956.

Is Laverne Baker talking about her hit "Tweedle Dee" or predicting her 1963 hit, "See See Rider?"

1956

never got to finish, the screams were so loud. This was the first real rock 'n' roll concert in Vancouver, and Haley was the first white artist to be accepted for his new music. Without question, Bill Haley deserves a lot of credit for putting rock 'n' roll on the map.

During my hour-long interview with Bill Haley, he mentioned that the spotlight would not be shining on him much longer. Referring to Elvis Presley, he said that "the hillbilly cat" from Memphis was going to be the real giant of rock 'n' roll.

In Haley's words, "Presley's got the looks, the talent, and the magic to make him very important in the months and years to come." Describing Elvis as a combination of Marlon Brando, Jimmy Dean, Hank Williams, and Frank Sinatra, Haley insisted that "the hillbilly cat" was the most significant new singer in the history of the record business and was going to rip the music world apart.

I went back to the radio station after the concert to do a show and hauled out the Presley releases available at that time. I played "That's Alright Mama" over and over again. The next day RCA's switchboard was jammed. Haley was right. The Presley kick was on!

Although the 1956 rock 'n' roll scene was dominated by Elvis, Canada made a contribution with the Four Lads. This Toronto-based group, which had a beautiful harmonic style, became well known when it backed up Johnnie Ray's hit "Little White Cloud That Cried." As a point of interest for trivia collectors, the original rendition of another Johnnie Ray hit, "Just Walking in the Rain," was recorded on Elvis Presley's old label, the Sun label, by the Prisonaires, who were prisoners in a jail in Tennessee. Johnnie Ray was the first white person who poured out emotion, showing bodily signs of torment and violence as he performed. To parents at the time, this was a no-no.

As 1956 rolled to a close, the news highlights reminded us that this was the year that wedding bells rang for Prince Rainier and Grace Kelly and for Marilyn Monroe and Arthur Miller. Sports fans were ecstatic to see Don Larsen of the New York Yankees pitch the first perfect ball game in the World Series. We talked about togetherness, blue jeans, bobby sox, charm bracelets, panty raids, Bridey Murphy and trading stamps.

But most of all we talked about rock 'n' roll. It was here to stay.

In those days, I shared billing with the movies.

Signing autographs at the 1956 premiere in Vancouver of Love Me Tender.

The guy in the middle is not a member of the Crew Cuts!

"I Love How You Love Me" was a hit by the Paris Sisters, who appeared in Vancouver in 1956.

Top Ten

1. *All Shook Up* — Elvis Presley
2. *Love Letters in the Sand* — Pat Boone
3. *Little Darlin'* — The Diamonds
4. *Young Love* — Tab Hunter
5. *So Rare* — Jimmy Dorsey
6. *Don't Forbid Me* — Pat Boone
7. *Singing the Blues* — Guy Mitchell
8. *Young Love* — Sonny James
9. *Too Much* — Elvis Presley
10. *Round and Round* — Perry Como

On Broadway

West Side Story
The Music Man
Look Back in Anger
The Dark at the Top of the Stairs
Look Homeward Angel (Pulitzer Prize winner, 1958)

On Television

Tonight Show
  (with Steve Allen)
Voice of Firestone
Twenty-One Quiz Show
  (with Charles Van Doren)
Phil Silvers Show
Mr. and Mrs. North
Julius LaRosa
  Dragnet
  (with Jack Webb)

Top Movies

The Bridge on the River Kwai
Peyton Place
Sayonara
Twelve Angry Men
Witness for the Prosecution
Raintree County
Funny Face
Pal Joey
The Prince and the Showgirl

The Oscars

Best Picture	*The Bridge on the River Kwai*
Best Director	David Lean *(The Bridge on the River Kwai)*
Best Actor	Alec Guinness *(The Bridge on the River Kwai)*
Best Supporting Actor	Red Buttons *(Sayonara)*
Best Actress	Joanne Woodward *(The Three Faces of Eve)*
Best Supporting Actress	Muyoshi Umeki *(Sayonara)*
Best Song	"All the Way" by James Van Heusen and Sammy Cahn from *The Joker Is Wild*

Best Sellers

Below the Salt
  Thomas B. Costain

On the Beach
  Neville Shute

The Hidden Persuaders
  Vance Packard

A Death in the Family
  James Agee (Pulitzer Prize winner, 1958)

Rally Round the Flag, Boys
  Max Shulman

1957

By 1957 rock 'n' roll was everywhere. We listened to rock 'n' roll on the radio in our homes and in our cars. We played the records on the most basic of record players and on the jukebox. Black and white television had become a permanent feature of living rooms and family rooms throughout North America.

New York-based journalist Ed Sullivan was now a TV host, and he quickly adapted his Sunday night national TV show to include the best and the loudest and even the worst of rock 'n' roll headliners for all of North America to see and enjoy.

For me, 1957 was a memorable year because I met and interviewed Elvis Presley, Buddy Holly and the Crickets, Frankie Avalon, Buddy Knox, the Everly Brothers, Paul Anka, Eddie Cochran, and many more artists as they toured Canada and the States.

Packaged rock shows were now racially mixed, and young people jammed theaters, auditoriums, and supper clubs across North America to enjoy their favorite artist in person — whether he or she was black or white didn't matter. Talent was what drew the crowds. The practice of having a white artist rerecord a hit made popular by a black artist was now being abandoned. Cover records were finished.

Country music was becoming more sophisticated, although it had a ways to go before reaching the sophistication of Dolly Parton, Willie Nelson, and other space-age Nashville-groomed recording stars. At this time, it became fashionable for those other than cowboys to enjoy the warmth and simplicity of country music.

At CKWX in Vancouver where I was now the host of the "Teen Canteen" show, I was receiving new record releases almost daily. One type of record I was not receiving was the pioneer-style 78 rpm record, which today is a collector's item. This heavy record was being replaced by the 45 rpm record, which had a huge hole in the middle and required a special spindle on radio station turntables and flimsy plastic insert adaptors for home record players.

Around this time, teenagers began hanging knitted dice from the rearview mirrors of their cars, which were often customized 1949 Fords. You could buy the dice in stores or specialty shops, but girls often made them for their boyfriends. Another bit of trivia: in 1957 a small toy company in Los Angeles introduced the Barbie Doll.

42 *Everyone loved his gold lamé jacket, but it was too heavy for Elvis. He stopped wearing the trousers and everyone copied his wide-leg pants.*

43 *Bruno Cimmoll, Vernon Presley, Mark Raines and I during the Vancouver press conference. Elvis looks to Colonel Parker for the correct answer.*

1957

From Toronto and California there emerged a talented group called the Diamonds. People thought they were black, but they were a white group who had recorded a "cover" record of "Little Darlin'," which was originally recorded by the Gladiolas. The Diamonds had been recording on the Mercury label for some time, but it was "Little Darlin'" that put them on the map.

Earlier, they had toured as a jazz group, but their devastating and hilarious sense of humor eventually terminated their career as serious progressive jazz musicians. They used to do a rock 'n' roll parody — it was the thing for non rock groups to make fun of Elvis and laugh at the shake, rattle, and roll of Haley and all the others. This part of the Diamonds' act was so successful, however, that they said goodbye to jazz and became rock 'n' rollers.

Earlier I mentioned that Harry Belafonte's *Calypso* album had broken sales records. It also triggered a fad in Caribbean music, food, clothes, and travel. Here was a black sex symbol singing a new type of folk song that the establishment hoped would replace rock 'n' roll.

The "Banana Boat Song," also known as "Day-O," was aired everywhere and appealed to eastern North Americans and to the monied set who could travel in the Caribbean. On the West Coast, Caribbean music was a real novelty, and when Belafonte appeared at the PNE forum in Vancouver the audience was spellbound and the critics approving. It was fashionable to enjoy Harry Belafonte because he wasn't a rock 'n' roller.

"Bye, Bye, Love" by the Everly Brothers was another winner in 1957 and came in at number 11 for the year. The Everly Brothers were bright and colorful and possessed an unusual ability to harmonize. I worked with them many times and enjoyed these talented brothers. Their parents had been in show business, and along the way they had met a husband and wife songwriting team, Boudleaux and Felice Bryant, who wrote "Bye, Bye, Love" and "Wake Up, Little Susie," among other hits. The latter was banned in Boston because of its suggestive lyrics. Today it's a classic.

Buddy Knox introduced the Tex-Mex sound with "Party Doll," which was number 13 for the year. Debbie Reynolds pleased the youngsters and the June-spoon set with "Tammy" from the movie

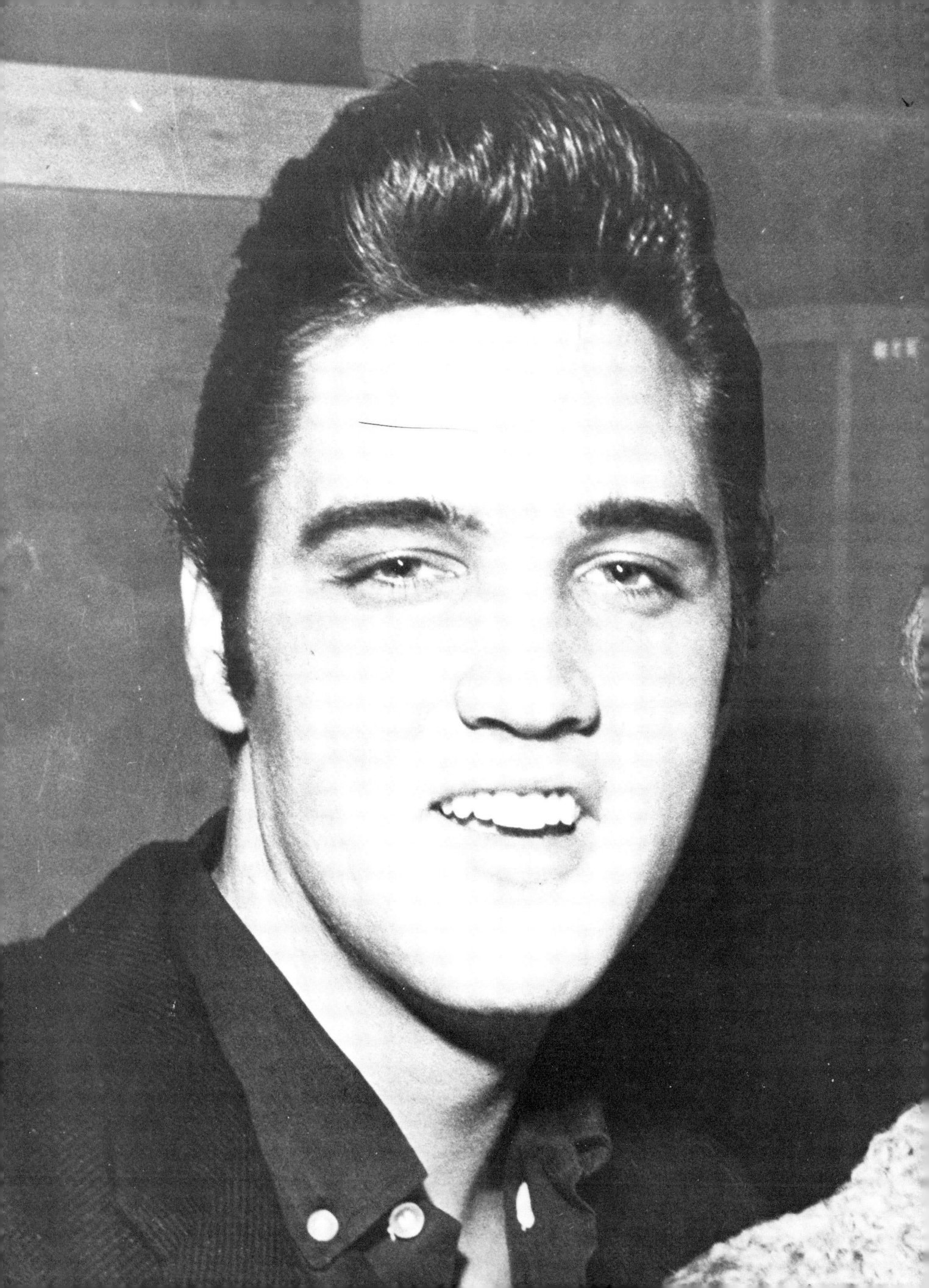

1957

by the same name. Young Rick Nelson, fresh from "Ozzie and Harriet," recorded "Be Bop Baby," which was a big hit in 1957. And Elvis? He was there in the solid 14 spot with "Teddy Bear," one of his many great recordings, featured in his second movie, Loving You.

When Marty Robbins sang "A White Sport Coat and a Pink Carnation," he not only appealed to record buyers throughout the continent but also started a trend among guys attending the high school proms and other teenage functions. Robbins had been recording on Columbia records, but others had also been recording his hit songs. The number seven song of the year, "Singing the Blues," which Guy Mitchell popularized, had been a hit on the country charts for Marty.

Remember "You Send Me" by Sam Cooke? Sam and his manager Bumps Blackwell, went to the top 100 radio stations across North America and introduced themselves to disc jockeys as a way of promoting Sam Cooke and getting his record played on the air. Believe me, it was effective.

I was on the air at CKWX one night when two men rang the doorbell, introduced themselves as Sam Cooke and Bumps Blackwell, and handed me a recording. I invited them in and put Sam on the air for an immediate interview. That was spontaneous radio — it doesn't happen very often today.

I played "You Send Me" and the flip side, which was "Summertime" from *Porgy and Bess*. The record took off, and Sam Cooke went on to great fame.

I was really impressed with Sam Cooke. He had great style and made a big impact on the record scene. Many young artists today learn about "soul" singing from the Sam Cooke of the fifties. One of his best-selling albums was *The Man Who Invented Soul*.

Frank Sinatra's one-time son-in-law Tommy Sands lucked out when he acted in a Kraft Music Hall television presentation called "Teenage Idol," an appearance that Elvis had turned down through his mentor, Colonel Tom Parker. During the TV show Tommy sang "Teenage Crush," which ended up being one of the big hits of the year. It sold one million copies in 48 hours and a few people speculated that Tommy would be another carbon of Elvis. (He wasn't.)

With Vernon Presley, "Teddy Bear," and Elvis. Vancouver, 1957.

1957

"Moonlight Gambler" kept Frankie Laine's voice booming over the radio. And Andy Williams came to everyone's attention for the first time without his brothers with a hit called "Butterfly." As for Fats Domino, that cat just never cooled off. He continued to be as strong an influence as he had been since 1950, and in 1957 his song "I'm Walkin' " appealed to both black and white audiences.

The "Show of Stars" held in Vancouver on October 23, 1957, was historic. The lineup included Frankie Lymon and the Teenagers, Buddy Holly and the Crickets, George Hamilton IV, Buddy Knox, Jimmy Bowen and the Rhythm Orchids, Don and Phil Everly, Paul Anka, and one of my idols, Eddie Cochran.

I was particularly anxious to meet Buddy Holly. He and the Crickets had their first ride up the charts to the number three spot in August 1957. "That'll Be the Day" captured everyone's feeling that summer. In those halcyon days of rock 'n' roll and pop radio, a deejay who loved the music would listen to every single new release that was distributed — both sides. I liked "That'll Be the Day" and played it for months before it ever made a mark on the national charts.

In those days, *Cash Box* magazine had a page filled with the Top 10 records from various deejays in North America. I was one of the few Canadians on that page. I had listed "That'll Be the Day" on my top list for six weeks running. In an interview, Buddy Holly later told me that it was my listing of the song that brought it to the attention of other radio stations in the United States and Canada.

In 1982, a record of Buddy Holly's songs and my interview with him was released in an album called *Visions of Buddy* with the original Crickets for the Great Northwest Music Company. The album is still selling all over North America to collectors who never forgot the man who entertained for only 18 months before he was killed in the same plane crash that hurtled Ritchie Valens and the "Big Bopper," J.P. Richardson, to their deaths in 1959. Side musician Waylon Jennings missed the flight.

Buddy Holly was a country boy with enthusiasm. He was happy to have a hit and was intent on becoming more successful. In the interview, I asked him what he had coming out. He said that he and his group had just recorded a new song called "Oh, Boy." It was an instant hit and rose to the Top 10 in *Billboard* magazine in 1957.

Eaton's Window Display, 1956.

Elvis with a friend

Vancouver press conference with Bruno Cimmoll and Elvis. The question Elvis was pondering was: "Where does an Elvis Presley vacation?" The answer he gave me: "Africa, I guess."

1957

Buddy Holly was a diamond in the rough. In the photograph of him in this chapter, you can see that his teeth had not yet been capped and his glasses were not as stylish as they would be later. He looked like an average blue-collar worker who might live down the street.

That didn't matter at all to his fans. Buddy was a star of unique talent. He had developed a sound unlike any other by incorporating some of Elvis Presley's grunts and groans and, some say, Erroll Garner's moans into his music. Buddy Holly and the Crickets filled that hall in Vancouver in October 1957, and, I'll tell you, we all recognized that evening as something quite extraordinary.

In later years, Buddy Holly would be described as the leader of the Tex-Mex sound that originated in the late fifties. Buddy Knox was another Tex-Mex originator. He was born in — are you ready? — Happy, Texas, and he was the "rockingest" of them all. His hit "Party Doll" was a raucous, hand-clapping, foot-stomping hit that was tremendous fun to dance to. Regrettably, Buddy's star rose and fell by about 1962, although he still appears around the world in small clubs.

My frenetically paced interviews with the guests on the "Show of Stars" included one with Eddie Cochran, who had come to enjoy national attention as a result of his appearance in the film *The Girl Can't Help It*. At the time, Eddie's career was in a bit of a slump. His recording of "Drive-In Show" was a regional hit in Vancouver, but it didn't catch on nationally. The following spring, however, Eddie came up with the unforgettable smash "Summertime Blues."

Eddie died in a taxi cab accident in England in April 1960. Had he lived, there is no doubt that he could have been one of the giants of the second wave of rock 'n' roll.

Another headliner at the Vancouver concert in 1957 was Paul Anka, who was a tender but dynamic 15 years of age at the time. During my interview with him, he projected an air of arrogance. Later I realized he was probably covering up an inferiority complex. He was, after all, the youngest guy on the program.

Paul Anka's own composition and recording "Diana" eventually propelled him to real stardom. He was the first to show the world that Canada could produce exceptionally talented recording stars. Although Canadians already had a big chunk of Hollywood

1957

sewn up, we didn't make a mark in the pop field until Paul Anka surfaced.

Over the years, Paul has written hundreds of hits he has sung himself. In addition, he has written an abundance of songs for other artists, including "My Way," which has become Frank Sinatra's trademark; "She's a Lady" for Tom Jones; and the "Tonight Show" theme, which signals the arrival of Johnny Carson into North American homes five nights a week.

In 1957 I also met Jimmy Bowen. Jimmy had met Buddy Knox and David Aldred in the midfifties, and they formed their own group, the Rhythm Orchids, with Jimmy on bass guitar, Buddy playing the lead, and David on drums. In January 1957, the Rhythm Orchids recorded "Party Doll," a Jimmy Bowen and Buddy Knox composition with Buddy Knox singing the lead. During that same session, Jimmy Bowen recorded "I'm Sticking with You." Both songs were released at the same time on separate singles and both became hits during the year.

Frankie Avalon was something of an anomaly on the "Show of Stars." Up to this point most rock 'n' roll hits had come from the South — places like Memphis, New Orleans, and Happy, Texas. Frankie's music was recorded by Chancellor Records in Philadelphia, and he was one of the first teen idols to be promoted on television through Dick Clark's "American Bandstand." This show made it possible for Philadelphia record companies to gain exposure.

"American Bandstand" swept across the United States and Canada. Every afternoon teenagers would hurry home from school, turn on the TV, and dance to the latest craze. They still do today, on Saturday mornings, as "American Bandstand" keeps everyone up to date on the latest dances, songs, and fads. From Little Rock Arkansas, to Vancouver, B.C. "American Bandstand" has set the standard for teenage style.

Frankie Avalon's greater fame was the result of a series of beach party movies he did with Mouseketeer Annette Funicello. To many, he was one of the more boring manufactured stars that were being packaged and labeled for the teenage market. But I'll give him credit — today you'll hear Frankie Avalon making a comeback at some of the better supper clubs across North America. He's been on television too, and he's aged very well.

Vancouver press conference with (from left) Bruno Cimmoli, Mark Raines, RCA rep Ernie Henn, Elvis's road manager Tom Diskin, Norm Pringle of CKDA Radio and Hugh Pickett of Famous Artists. Tom Diskin rarely appeared in photographs.

Elvis Impersonators on stage at the Orpheum Theatre. Vancouver, 1957.

Jiving at the Kitsilano Showboat celebration. Summer, 1957.

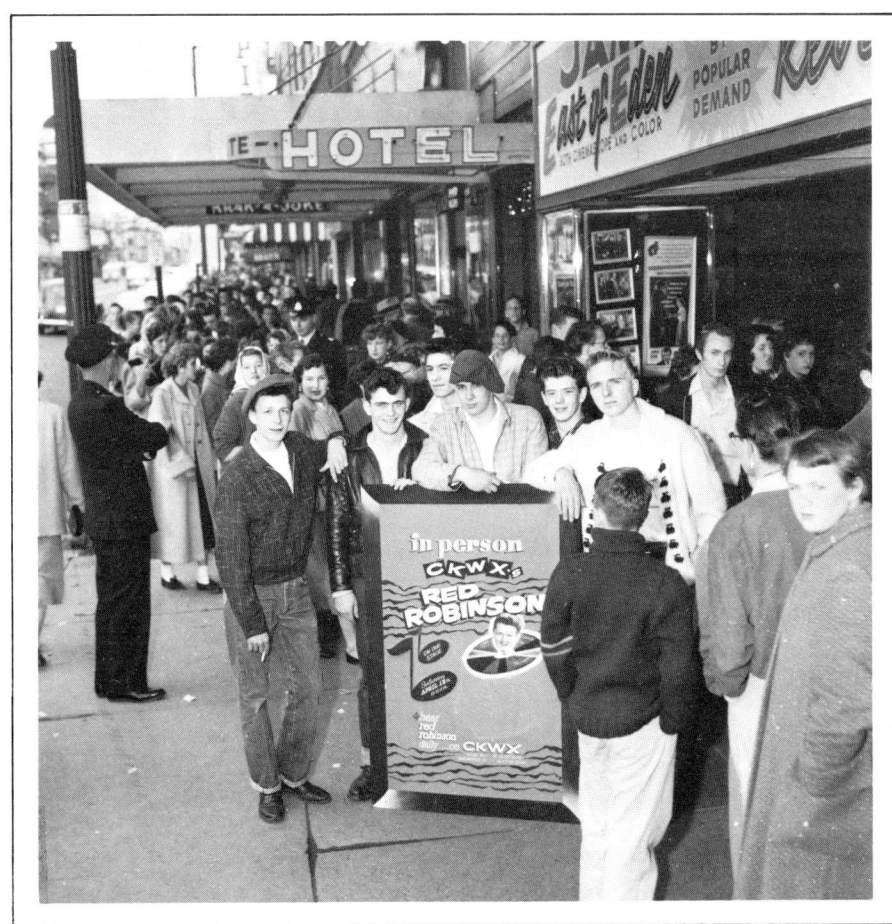

Interviewing theatre-goers during East of Eden *and* Rebel without a Cause *double feature.*

1957

As for Frankie Lymon and the Teenagers — also on the "Show of Stars" — the success of the 1956 hit "Why Do Fools Fall in Love?" was the first of many for the group on the pop parade. Tragically, Frankie Lymon died of a drug overdose in 1968.

In 1957, you could find recordings to suit every taste — gospel, rockabilly, calypso, folk, pop, novelty, country, rhythm and blues, easy-listening, classical, and jazz. On the West Coast, running counterpoint to the rock 'n' roll movement, was the influence of the jazz groups. Coffee houses were crammed with jazz fans listening to the top musicians in the business.

In the meantime, radio was undergoing significant changes. Top 40 was new. No longer was radio an enclave for soap operas and shows with limited appeal and changeable formats. Radio station owners began demanding better sound, more successful sponsors, ratings, and a consistent sound twenty-four hours a day. The practice of broadcasting only until dusk was also ending.

A Midwestern radio station owner, Todd Storz, noticed that although there were 100 selections on the jukebox at his favorite hangout, everyone played the same 10 or 20 all the time. He began playing only these favorites on the station he owned and was immediately successful. This was the beginning of Top 40 radio as we know it today. A brewer, Gordon McLendon, applied this concept to KLIF in Dallas and achieved the first major market exposure for Top 40 radio.

There was a whole lot of shakin' going on with Jerry Lee Lewis, who had been discovered by Sam Phillips, owner of Sun Records in Tennessee. Phillips was no slouch; he had originally signed Elvis to a record contract. Those records are collector's items today. Elvis was later lured away to RCA records on advice from Colonel Tom Parker. He remained with RCA until his death. Today, records continue to be released from the vast store of material owned by RCA.

Jerry Lee Lewis could be called a white Little Richard. He was a real dynamo on stage and is still prominent in the music world today. In those days, he hit paydirt with "A Whole Lot of Shakin' Going On" and "Great Balls of Fire."

Another marvel who rose to the top but wasn't a rock 'n' roller

1957

was Johnny Mathis. He had two giant hits — "Chances Are" and "It's Not for Me to Say." Then there was Nat "King" Cole, who reluctantly offered some rhythm and blues in 1957 with a hit called "Send for Me." Nat was irked at Capitol for insisting on this song, he told me during his Vancouver visit in 1958.

Some British hits were creeping onto the music charts in North America. Russ Hamilton had a big song called "Rainbow." Little did we know that seven years later Britain would become a major force in North American entertainment.

Regional record hits are always a boost for those starting out. Such was the case with singer Jimmie Rodgers of Camus, Washington, about seven miles from Portland, Oregon. A performer by the name of Chuck Miller, who recorded "The House of Blue Lights" in 1955, discovered Rodgers. Chuck used to come to Vancouver, and in addition to his night club appearances, he would play gigs for me at lunchtime hops at selected high schools.

In 1957, he brought me a demo record by this new singer. The record was "Honeycomb," and you can guess the rest. The flip side was something called "Woman from Liberia." Because of North American hostility toward the Soviet Union in the fifties, Liberia was chosen to replace Siberia, which had originally been used in the song.

Jimmie Rodgers went on to have many hits, and he even had his own television show in the late fifties. His folk music was similar to that of Pete Seeger and the Weavers, who had been popular in the late forties and early fifties and are still popular on campuses across North America. But while many Seeger folk songs carried messages, preceding the heavier tunes by Bob Dylan, Joan Baez, Judy Collins and a host of other folk singers, Jimmie Rodgers's songs were addressed to a more family-oriented, homogeneous audience.

Despite the popularity of these stars and their songs, Elvis still had a stranglehold on the Hit Parade, which was rapidly becoming known as the Top 40. When *Jailhouse Rock* was released as a movie and an album, every record and movie company in North America and England was running around trying to capture their version of an Elvis Presley. They didn't succeed.

By far the single most important event of my life happened in 1957. This event was shared by millions of fans in North America as Elvis Presley toured the United States and Canada.

With Buddy Knox and Jimmy Bowen in 1957.

Chatting with Fats Domino at the Denman Auditorium in Vancouver, 1957.

Record-breaking crowds joined us at Kitsilano Showboat celebration in Vancouver, 1957.

Another Eaton's "Theme for Teens" fan club display, downtown Vancouver.

1957

Elvis appeared outside of the United States only three times in his entire life — in 1957 he made three separate trips to Ottawa, Toronto and Vancouver. Despite attempts to seduce him to perform in Europe, Britain, Australia and the Orient, Elvis Presley's sole appearances outside the States were in Canada.

In 1956 I had tried to book Elvis Presley into Vancouver, but I was unsuccessful. At the time, Elvis was busy shooting the movie *Jailhouse Rock*. But when the movie was concluded, Elvis did do a tour and, happily, Vancouver was on the circuit.

When the deal was put together, I wasn't the one who booked Elvis into Vancouver. A friend of mine, Hugh Pickett of Famous Artists, working with Seattle entrepreneur Zollie Volchuck, got the booking.

It was arranged that I would meet Elvis and interview him the day of his performance. At twelve noon, I mustered with Knox Coupland and Ernie Henn of RCA, along with Zollie Volchuck, in the lobby of Vancouver's Georgia Hotel. We rode the elevator together to the twelfth floor and started walking toward the room assigned to Elvis. Later, on CKWX, I made the mistake of mentioning Elvis's room number, 1226, on the air, and chaos resulted when a gaggle of groupies broke into his room and stole souvenirs and some of his private possessions.

As we continued along the hallway, a burly former U.S. Marine Corps Sergeant stopped us; only after Zollie explained who we were, were we allowed to continue. All of Elvis's guards were former U.S. Marines employed by Colonel Tom Parker to protect his boy.

Then came the moment I had been waiting for. The door opened and Tom Diskin, Elvis's road manager, introduced us to Elvis. At first, everything seemed a bit strained. But once Elvis heard that I was an enthusiastic fan, he relaxed and became most cordial.

When people ask me what I thought of Elvis, I have to answer that I found him polite, shy and charming. He was very soft-spoken and there was nothing pretentious about the man. I guess one of the main reasons I have always been a Presley fan is that when I met him he was down-to-earth and seemingly unaffected by his incredible success.

1957

Elvis lounged on the bed, strode up and down the room and seemed quite energetic even though he was supposed to be resting up for his press conference and concert that night.

I stayed for about an hour and a half. Just before I left, an attractive young brunette — similar in appearance to Priscilla Presley — entered the room. She was, as I recall, a paid companion, and she was very pretty and very unobtrusive. Since nothing more has ever been heard about her, it also appears that she was very discreet.

That evening, as I was on my way to the Elvis Presley press conference in the coaching area of Vancouver's Empire Stadium, I bought two buttons from the concessionaires, who were doing a landslide business. One read "I like Elvis" and the other, "I hate Elvis." I flipped them over and discovered that both had an Elvis Presley identification mark on them — the Colonel didn't miss a beat when he was promoting his boy.

That press conference was chaos. Newsmen, reporters, radio people and TV cameramen packed the area.

One reporter, Mark Raines, later a member of Canada's Parliament, fired questions about Elvis's likes and dislikes as reported in the gossip magazines. Elvis obviously didn't appreciate Mark's line of questioning and became a bit annoyed. But the press was always looking for a sensational story.

One of the photographs in this chapter shows how we all crowded around Elvis. What you can't see is Elvis hunched down on his knees on top of a large coffee table. He remained that way for over 40 minutes, shifting now and then from one leg to another. Clearly Elvis was in excellent shape.

As Elvis faced the sea of reporters, he would look over their heads to Colonel Tom Parker, who was just behind the bank of press and media reps. When Elvis wasn't sure how he should answer a question, he would look in the direction of the Colonel, who would nod or shake his head accordingly. Then, and only then, would Elvis answer the question.

This was brilliant strategy. Elvis had a disarming way of "shooting from the hip" when he answered questions with no guidance. This way, he could both appear spontaneous and answer with discretion.

Frankie Avalon was one of the leaders at the 1957 "Show of Stars."

With Little Richard at the CKWX studios in 1957 during one of his more subdued moments.

Eddie Cochran shows me how to play the guitar, 1957.

Clyde McPhatter was a marvelous entertainer. At CKWX in 1957.

1957

At one point, I hopped up on the table with Elvis and kneeled down beside him in the same position he had been maintaining for over 40 minutes. I decided that since I had taken all the abuse for playing rock 'n' roll music on the radio from that same group of reporters, I might as well try and hog the scene and get the best damn interview I could.

Twenty-five years later, on the anniversary of Elvis's appearance in Vancouver, even the skeptics were phoning me for interviews to commemorate the 1957 press conference and spectacular show.

Because I was the emcee of the show, I was able to remain with Elvis after the rest of the reporters had been discharged. He was restless — a bundle of nervous energy. He had a nervous twitch and was constantly toying with his wristwatch and twisting the expansion bracelet. There was nothing to do in that waiting area except chat.

Our topics of conversation included comparison of our boyhoods (we each grew up poor), the changing world, our families, his love of rhythm and blues, country music, and gospel music and the normal things that two young men would talk about anywhere. Elvis also said that he hoped the whole rock 'n' roll scene would not lose its fire. He said he wanted to continue to perform as long as it was possible.

In addition, he asked me all kinds of questions about my CKWX radio show, the kids who listened and how they reacted to his TV appearances, and his records. I answered as honestly and as clearly as I could — remember, I too, was a fan and terribly in awe of the man.

Finally, Elvis walked to the door and invited one of the many policemen guarding the hallway to come into the room. He asked to borrow the cop's handcuffs. Then he beckoned me over to the side of the room — by this time we were in the B.C. Lions' dressing room — and handcuffed me to the shower rod. Then he hid the key and laughed like a madman. Yes, I was nervous — what if he decided the joke was so good that he'd leave me there? He asked me how I'd get out. I joked with him for a while. I was sweating, but I decided to appear cool.

1957

There was a knock on the door and someone said it was time for me to go on and start the show. Elvis looked over to where I was standing, rather uncomfortably, and laughed and undid the handcuffs.

Just before I got set to head for the stage, Elvis stretched out his hand and said, "It was nice meeting you. Good luck with your radio career and I hope we get to see each other again down the road."

That was Elvis Presley, talking to me on August 31, 1957, just before his 8:00 p.m. appearance at Empire Stadium in Vancouver.

Except for a telephone call later that night, I never spoke to Elvis Presley again.

My heart was pounding with excitement as I walked toward the stage. The Jordanaires, a gospel group from the south who had recently been added to the background sound of Elvis's RCA recordings, were the last warm-up act that night. The band included Bill Black on bass, D. J. Fontana on drums, and Scotty Moore, who played an incredible guitar.

As they concluded their act, I got set to step out in front of more than 25,000 fans, all screaming for Elvis. I had been briefed by Tom Diskin, Elvis's road manager, to point to the west side of the stadium when I introduced Elvis. Elvis was then to come running out of the tunnel and step into a large black Cadillac limousine convertible, with the top down. My introduction was brief. An off-stage announcer shouted my name as emcee. Then I walked out to the thundering applause and said, "On behalf of the 'Teen Canteen,' Canada's largest teen show, I'm proud tonight to present to you, Elvis Presley."

With that announcement, I pointed to my right, and Elvis came running out of the tunnel and hopped into his waiting limousine. The crowd went berserk. It sounded like a city of a million all screaming and yelling in unison.

Elvis was wearing the jacket of his solid gold lamé suit, black pants, and a black shirt. Earlier I had asked him why he didn't wear the whole suit. He explained the creases made them look terrible and, furthermore, it was too hot. The gold lamé suit had been Colonel Parker's idea. Here was the golden boy of music in the fifties, and the Colonel was going to have him appear in gold — real gold — to show the world just how big his boy was. The Colonel knew the value of glamour, and he used it masterfully.

At the CKWX control panel, 1957.

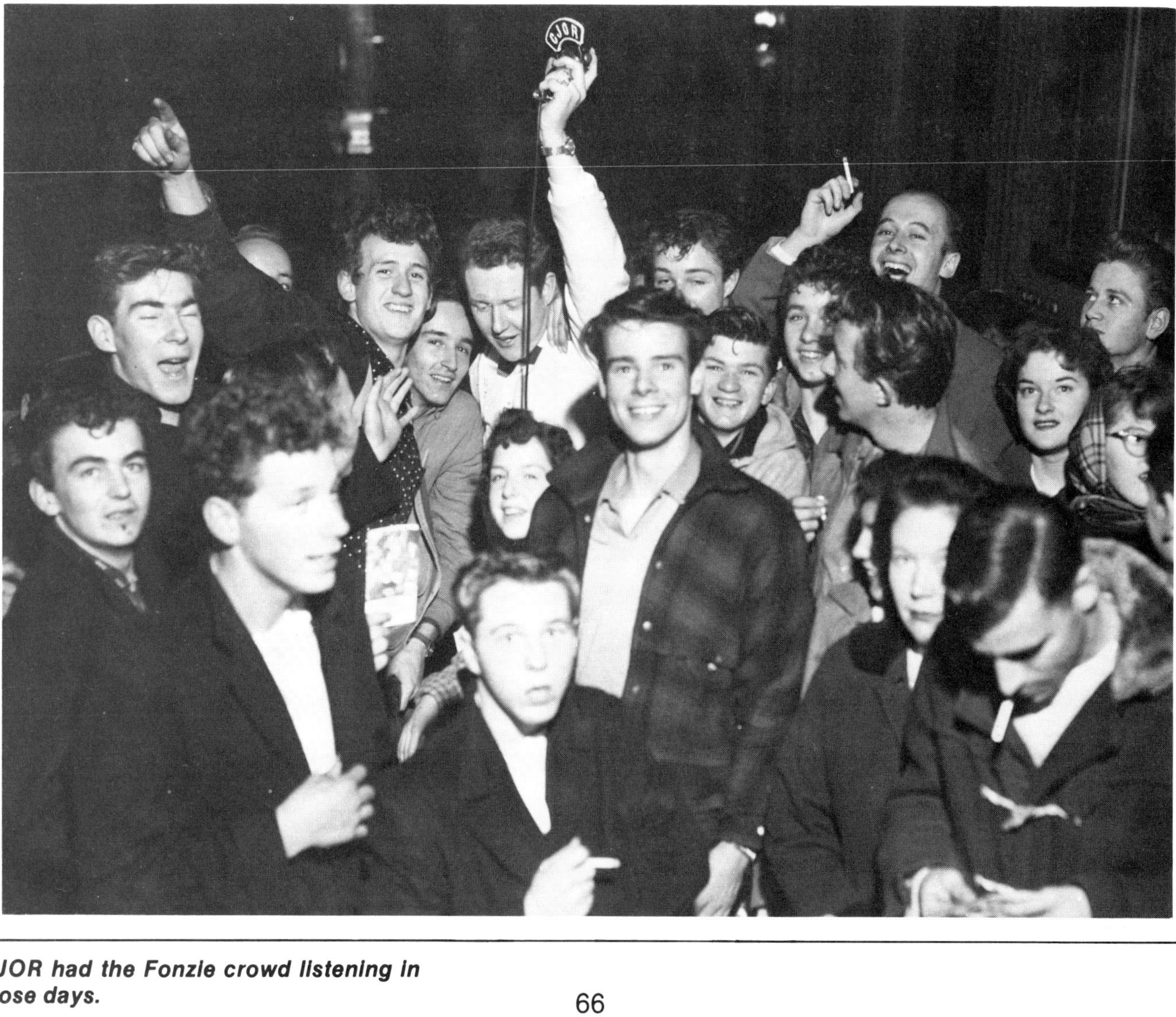

CJOR had the Fonzie crowd listening in those days.

"You ain't nothin' but a Hound Dog."

Candid shots of Elvis

Photos courtesy Barbara Dobie

A collection of Elvis snapshots . . .

1957

the world just how big his boy was. The Colonel knew the value of glamour, and he used it masterfully.

As the limousine drove slowly around the stadium, each section went wild. (My tapes have been bootlegged all over the world, and my own records are available to attest to the excitement.) Finally, Elvis ran up on the stage. He chattered to the crowd, made fun of himself — Elvis had a superb sense of humour — and sang some of his hot hits of the day, including "Hound Dog." Elvis was the consummate showman and his show was magnificent.

At the conclusion of the show, Elvis rushed out and handed one of his "Memphis Mafia" — his pals who acted as "gofers" — his gold lamé jacket. We both were shoved down a trapdoor to an area beneath the stage, and we remained there until the crowd dispersed. Meanwhile, the guy wearing the jacket ran for the limousine, which was parked behind the stage. He hopped in and was driven toward the players' tunnel, where Elvis had sprung from at the beginning of the show. The crowd was rushing onto the field by this time and ran for the limo for one last look. The fake Elvis then jumped out of the limo — he must have been terrified — and ran for the tunnel, the crowd running behind him.

When the excitement had died down, Elvis and I came out from under the stage and Elvis walked quite casually to another car and was driven with no fanfare to downtown Vancouver. I describe this scenario to demonstrate Colonel Tom Parker's incredible organization and imagination.

I drove back to CKWX and went on the air to do my show at 10:00 p.m. I then proceeded to play every song Elvis had ever recorded up to that time. Around 2:30 a.m., my private line rang. It was Elvis, who thanked me and said goodbye.

It was a thrilling evening and one of my fondest memories of rock 'n' roll.

The legend of the fifties. My favorite picture of Buddy Holly, taken in 1957.

Top Ten Hits

1. *Nel Blu Dipinto Di Blu (Volare)* — Domenico Modugno
2. *All I Have to Do Is Dream* — The Everly Brothers
3. *Don't, I Beg of You* — Elvis Presley
4. *Witch Doctor* — David Seville
5. *Patricia* — Perez Prado
6. *Sail Along Silvery Moon* — Billy Vaughn
7. *Catch a Falling Star* — Perry Como
8. *Tequilla* — The Champs
9. *It's All in the Game* — Nat "King" Cole
10. *Return to Me* — Dean Martin

Grammy Awards

Record of the Year	*"Nel Blu Dipinto Di Blu" ("Volare")* (Domenico Modugno)
Song of the Year	
Album of the Year	*The Music from Peter Gunn* (Henry Mancini)
Best Male Vocalist	*Perry Como* ("Catch a Falling Star")
Best Female Vocalist	*Ella Fitzgerald* (The Irving Berlin Song Book)
Best Vocal Group	*Louis Prima and Keely Smith* ("That Old Black Magic")

Top Movies

Gigi
Auntie Mame
Cat on a Hot Tin Roof
The Defiant Ones
Separate Tables
I Want to Live
Some Came Running
Houseboat
South Pacific
The Old Man and the Sea

The Oscars

Best Picture	*Gigi*
Best Director	Vincente Minnelli *(Gigi)*
Best Actor	David Niven *(Separate Tables)*
Best Actress	Susan Hayward *(I Want to Live)*
Best Supporting Actor	Burl Ives *(The Big Country)*
Best Supporting Actress	Wendy Hiller *(Separate Tables)*
Best Song	"*Gigi*" by Frederick Loewe and Alan Jay Lerner from *Gigi*

On Broadway

Say Darling
The World of Susie Wong
Flower Drum Song
La Plume de ma Tante
Two for the Seesaw

On Television

Dragnet
   (with Jack Webb)
Douglas Fairbanks
Andy Williams
Mickey Rooney
The Honeymooners
Name That Tune
Amos 'n' Andy

Best Sellers

Doctor Zhivago
   Boris Pasternak

From the Terrace
   John O'Hara

Exodus
   Leon M. Uris

The Affluent Society
   John Kenneth Galbraith

Kids Say the Darndest Things
   Art Linkletter

Lolita
   Vladimir Nabokov

1958

Although rock 'n' roll continued to be controversial, it softened a little in 1958. Now my studio interviews included Gene Vincent, Bonnie Guitar, and Rick Nelson, all of whom had hits in 1958.

By the end of the fifties, radio was emerging as a force to be reckoned with. Except for the occasional variety show or family sitcom, television ignored the teen market.

Part of the appeal of radio back then was that it could be enjoyed in cars. In those days, before there were many options, riding around in cars was one way for teenagers to escape the surveillance of their parents.

Radio was a direct form of rebellion, and it was the forum that launched rock. Today that forum has been replaced by huge concerts, which you attend in person and then enjoy again on television.

Because of radio's teen appeal and its imaginative delivery, many young men and women wanted to become broadcasters. In most instances, men were hired for on-air activities as disc jockies, while women provided the backup in programming, promotion, and other areas. This unfortunate division of labor has changed considerably today.

Until the late fifties, rock 'n' roll was also strictly a male enclave. One of the first white women to make any kind of statement in rock 'n' roll was Connie Francis. In November 1957, Connie recorded the 1923 Harry Ruby-Bert Kalmer-Ted Snyder vaudeville classic, "Who's Sorry Now?" It became a million seller for MGM Records and instantly put Connie, who had been an obscure singer up until that time, into the big time. She had not wanted to record the song but had done so at her father's insistence, since "Who's Sorry Now?" was one of his favorite songs. By early 1958 it was high on the charts. In 1959 Connie followed it up with three hits, which included "My Happiness," "Lipstick on Your Collar," and "Among My Souvenirs," a song that dated back to 1927. In the sixties, she starred in three movies, *Where the Boys Are*, *Follow the Boys*, and *When the Boys Meet the Girls*.

Connie appeared in Vancouver in 1958 with a very great entertainer, Nat "King" Cole, whose list of hits spans the forties, fifties and sixties. He was the perfect gentleman. During his Vancouver

1958

appearance, Nat confided to me that he hated rock 'n' roll. That didn't lessen his appeal for me. When he died on February 15, 1965, of cancer, we lost a giant in the record industry and in popular music.

Throughout 1958, talent agencies and even some radio stations believed that if you ignored it, rock 'n' roll might go away. Mitch Miller, then artists and repertoire (A & R) chief of Columbia Records, made a speech in 1958 denouncing rock 'n' roll. Hearing of this, Allan Freed, the New York disc jockey, became annoyed and decided to ban all Columbia recordings from his radio show. Some of the major networks, including the powerful Mutual network, were also banning — or trying to ban — rock 'n' roll. Like anything else in life, once you ban it, the subject becomes even more popular.

In 1958, Conway Twitty recorded "It's Only Make Believe," his first international hit. Sheb Wooley came out with a novelty song called "Purple People Eater." The Silhouettes sang advice in "Get a Job" and the Everly Brothers gave us a great dance-and-drive tune with "Bird Dog."

Out of Philadelphia came a terrific stomper that made every wallflower ache for a partner. It was called "At the Hop," performed by Danny and the Juniors. Leiber and Stoller, two very important and prolific songwriters of the fifties, wrote and produced "Yakety Yak," which the Coasters recorded. Those Diamonds — the guys who gave up progressive jazz — recorded "The Stroll," and Duane Eddy put out an instrumental number called "Rebel Rouser" that launched his career.

Before going into the army, Elvis had prerecorded a lot of material that was timed for release during his tenure in Germany — clever thinking on the part of Elvis and the Colonel. One of his hits in 1958 was "Wear My Ring around Your Neck," a sentimental tune with a driving beat that reflected the feelings of thousands of other American servicemen who were drafted away from their sweethearts.

"Tequila," by the Champs, turned out to be one of the great instrumentals of the year. Dave Burgess was the lead performer; shouting the chorus "Tequila" were Jim Seals and Dash Crofts, who originally backed up Glen Campbell and his first band. Glen filled in as guitarist with the Champs on tour.

Although New York, Nashville and Los Angeles continued to

With Connie Francis in 1958. She was a lovely lady and a total pro.

The Stripes play Vancouver.

Red Robinson Canadian Bandstand Show.

Jimmy Morrison, Gerry Fiander, The Four Quarters, The Stripes, 1958.

1958

dominate the music scene, other areas began providing talent as well. Dick Clark and "American Bandstand" had been originating innovative music styles in Philadelphia and now the West Coast was providing a fresh outpouring of talent as well. "Willie and the Hand Jive" by Johnny Otis was one West Coast winner in 1958. Today that song is popular with aerobic dancers and daytime exercise shows.

Jerry Lee Lewis was causing quite a stir in 1958. His music and his antics were already receiving international attention when he announced quite casually in Britain that he had married his 14-year-old cousin, Myra Brown. The British press was outraged. The word spread across the Atlantic to this continent and instantly his recording of "High School Confidential" from the movie of the same name was banned by all white stations in North America. Jerry Lee Lewis's career came crashing down and he never totally recovered from this incident.

A popular rhythm and blues song that year was "What Am I Living For?" by Chuck Willis. This song has been done by many performers over the years. Ironically, Chuck died that year, on April 10, after a serious operation.

Young Bobby Darin appeared regularly with Dick Clark and, as a result, gained a lot of exposure in Canada and the United States. Do you remember "Splish Splash (I Was Taking a Bath)"? That was Bobby's contribution to music in 1958 — he wrote it and performed it. He also wrote "Early in the Morning" for Buddy Holly.

Bobby Darin's real name was Walden Robert Cassotto. He was walking down the street one day, thinking about a name change, and looked up at the sign in front of a Chinese restaurant. It had the word "Mandarin" in it. He decided he liked the last two syllables and Bobby Darin became his name.

Two performers who never appeared on "American Bandstand" were Rick Nelson and Elvis Presley. Rick didn't appear because he was a regular feature on his parents' nationally televised sitcom, "Ozzie and Harriet." At that time, the networks didn't encourage cross-promotion.

As for Elvis, Colonel Tom Parker was wise enough to realize that overexposure would kill the appeal of his boy. During his stint in the army, however, Elvis did do a telephone interview directly from Germany that was broadcast live on "American Bandstand."

1958

I can't stress enough the importance of "American Bandstand." All the young artists who were ambitious and wanted recognition rushed to Philadelphia to try and get a break. It was an interim period for rock 'n' roll; everything seemed to be in a holding pattern while the King was off the continent.

In addition to television in the late fifties, the introduction of the transistor radio was an important development. We all take radio for granted now, but in those days the transistor radio was a novelty. Between your car radio and your transistor, you could have unlimited entertainment. The transistor changed everything. You could put it in your hip pocket and go anywhere. Today, of course, the transistor has been upstaged by such variations as the Sony Walkman.

How did the transistor affect rock 'n' roll? The increased exposure to rock 'n' roll meant a massive increase in record sales. Frankie Lymon and the Teenagers sang about the transistor radio and Freddy Cannon had a hit of sorts in 1961 called "Transistor Sister."

Another electronic breakthrough was the introduction of stereo on records. Stereo sound had been invented several years before, but in 1958 the process was perfected to cut a left and right channel into a vinyl phonograph recording. What a difference this made!

Despite this breakthrough, however, it was several years before the average person had anything more than "hi-fi" in his or her living room. The set for playing stereo recordings was simply too expensive. What most people did was play the new, lush-sounding records on mono and forever wreck them for stereo when they finally acquired a true stereo record player. In those days, however, records were not as expensive and I think people just expected to replace them. What a shock it was to learn that many of the masters were not kept by the major recording companies, or that they were lost or destroyed by fires.

The same thing happened with older movies and early television shows. Amazingly, cans and cans of master cuts were either reused for another show or thrown out. Fortunately, I have always saved records, tapes, books and mementoes, and I now have an enormous collection.

Meanwhile, good old Hollywood was trying vainly to jump on the rock 'n' roll bandwagon and revive sagging box office receipts.

On November 22, 1958, Ritchie Valens appeared in Vancouver. Only 90 days later he was killed in a plane crash.

Appearing at the Gene Vincent show in Vancouver was Bonnie Guitar (middle), with me and Bill Davis, CKWX.

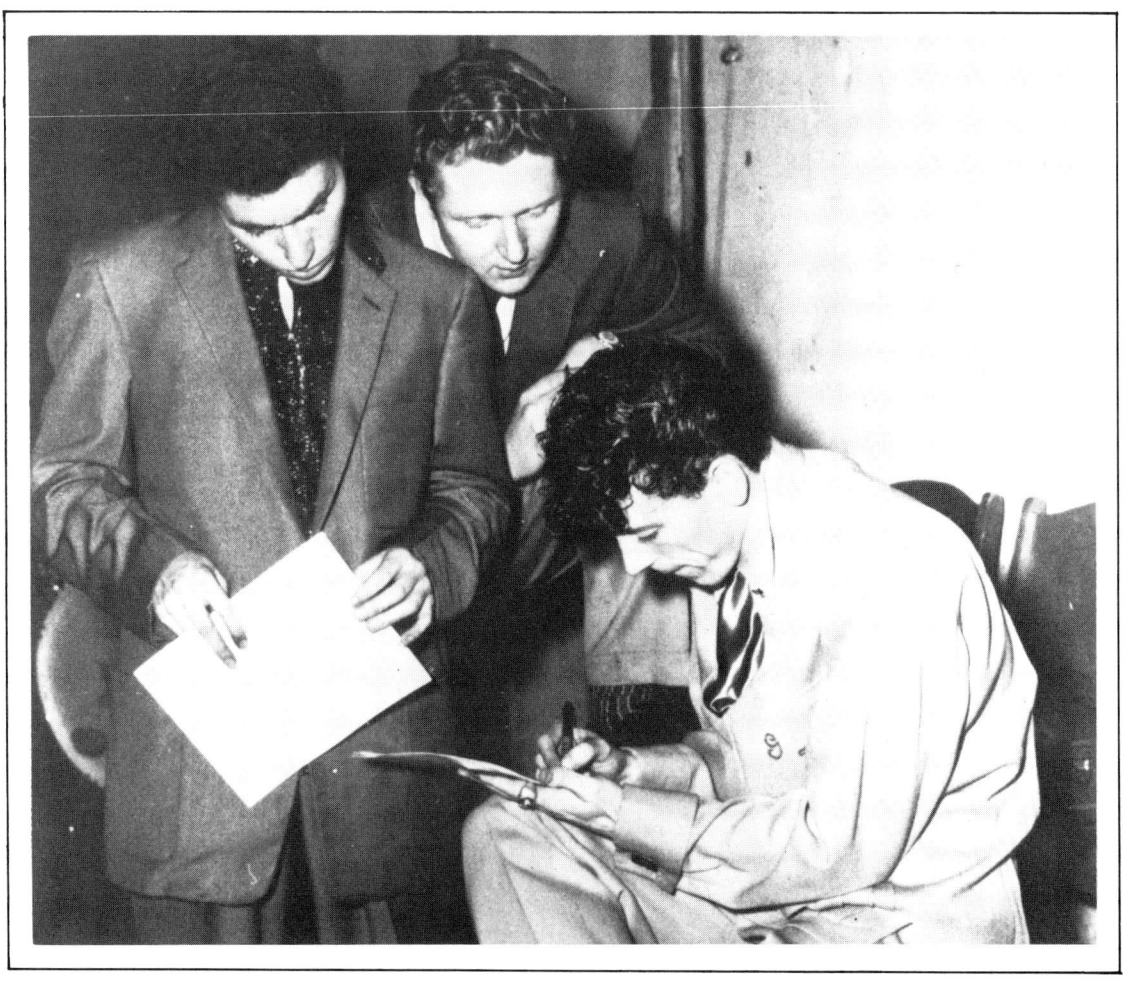

"Stripe's" guitarist Gerry Fiander and Gene Vincent on the right, 1958.

Red with Robin Luke, 1958.

Interviewing Ricky Nelson, Portland

1958

Tommy Sands, Pat Boone, Gary Crosby and others starred in *Mardi Gras*. Elvis burst onto the screen again with *King Creole*, which also starred Dean Jagger, Carolyn Jones and Walter Matthau. In the movie Elvis sang "Lover Doll" and "Hard-Headed Woman," which quickly reestablished him as a top box-office draw.

One guy who really had all the components of stardom and failed to capitalize on them was Rick Nelson. Rick made his first appearance in Vancouver in the spring of 1958 at the PNE Garden Auditorium. He didn't exactly receive the "personality" award at that performance. The late *Vancouver Sun* columnist Jack Wasserman wrote:

> When rock and roller Ricky Nelson finished his concert (?) a phalanx of bodyguards led by footballer Paul Cameron grabbed his arms and half dragged him to a waiting car. He was out of the building within ten seconds. Disc Jockey Red Robinson, the boy most responsible for local rock and roll, was booed down when he tried to introduce Nelson for the second show. Nelson came on stage unannounced. You couldn't hear a word Nelson said or sang. The kids screamed through every number. But, at the end of each number, the silence was almost eerie.
>
> There was no applause. Between shows, Nelson was whisked over to the neighboring Admiral Hotel for a shower. Trying to get back into the Gardens a mob of about 100 kids started grabbing and punching. They bowled over Nelson's burly bodyguards and the only man between Nelson and dismemberment was Famous Artists' Hugh Pickett, who has fewer muscles than anyone. He pulled Nelson to safety.

It was one of the most embarrassing shows I had ever emceed. Rick had this habit of gulping down Cokes on stage during his performance. Drinking Coke is not bad — but on stage? He did not

1958

have a dynamic on-stage personality and failed to project any kind of charisma. This audience had seen Bill Haley and the Comets and Elvis Presley's stellar performance, so Nelson's antics did not impress them in the least.

The screaming *during* his singing was a put-on rather than the natural emotional outburst that occurred during concerts by Elvis Presley and, later, the Beatles. Let me tell you, the Vancouver audience was left with a bad taste.

It's sad about Rick Nelson. He is a nice person, but he did not have the magnetism necessary for rock 'n' roll. His music, especially the work of his lead guitarist, James Burton, was some of the finest "white" rock 'n' roll.

In 1959, I met Rick Nelson again in Portland, Oregon, during the Oregon Centennial Exposition. During this show, he was well received by the audience. He had matured since the previous year and now had a sincerity that compensated for his lack of stage presence. One thing you cannot dispute — the man was so handsome that people compared him to Elvis!

A lot of Vancouver people remember March 31, 1958, as the day I got my come-uppance for a stunt I pulled with another wild man, former newscaster Jim McDonald. His antics could fill three volumes.

I went on the air that evening and started broadcasting news reports that a large whale had been washed up at Sunset Beach in downtown Vancouver. McDonald faked some on-the-scene reports from a phone in another part of the CKWX radio building and we created an exciting commentary on the alleged whale. We wanted to see if the gag was working, so Jim went down to the beach — a three-block sprint — and phoned to tell me that a lot of cars were jamming the shoreline.

He continued his on-the-spot reports with witty and colorful commentary — all fiction, of course. By midnight thousands of people were at the beach probing the waterfront with their car headlights to see the whale that wasn't there. At precisely midnight, I put "A Whale of a Tale" on the turntable. When it had finished, I said, "That's 'A Whale of a Tale' with Kirk Douglas and you have been taken in by a whale of an April Fool's joke." (Yes, Kirk put out a disc on Decca

1958

Records.) Jim and I continued to explain that it was a spoof and thanked everyone for joining in the fun.

It was only a matter of minutes before the beach mob came screaming toward the station; started pounding on the door, which, thankfully, was locked; and demanded to see me. I stayed put. The newsmen went out to pacify the crowd and learned that one party had driven 96 kilometers (58 miles) in a cab to see this whale that did not exist. In those days, before whales were commonly displayed in public aquariums and maritime shows, seeing a whale was a unique experience.

A most serious consequence had developed. The aquarium curator had left his bed and driven in his nightclothes to the site of the invisible whale to try and protect it. When he learned of the prank, he was furious and called the station manager. Unable to contact him, the curator found the assistant manager, who drove to CKWX, walked in and fired me on the spot.

I was only 21 and I was very upset, so I went into the men's washroom and threw up. All I had wanted to do was have some fun on the evening of April Fool's Day.

The next morning my phone rang at home. It was the station manager, Frank "Tiny" Elphicke, a giant of a man. Now I was really nervous. He asked me to come down to the station and meet him in his office. When he asked me how many people had showed up at the beach for my little prank, I admitted that I didn't know. He reached into his drawer, pulled out a police report, and read: "The Vancouver Police Department estimates the crowd at fifteen thousand."

He rose from his desk and extended his hand. I figured this was the kiss-off for real. Instead, he said, "What are you going to do to top that stunt?"

I always admired "Tiny" Elphicke but never more than that day. I was relieved to be back on the job. I continued to dream up stunts and pranks to draw attention to my show and the station, but I was a little more cautious until 1964, when . . . well, you can read about that incident in the 1964 chapter.

In addition to being a disc jockey, I also booked acts into British Columbia and the Pacific Northwest region of the United States. In October 1958, I booked 16-year-old Robin Luke, who was

1958

living in Hawaii, where his first recording, "Susie Darling," had taken off. He was signed to Dot Records after two vacationing record guys heard his local disc in Hawaii. Robin had written the song for his babysitter Susie. It was his one and only hit, although he did have a regional success with "My Girl." Norm N. Nite's book, *Rock On*, reports that Robin is now a college professor in Norfolk, Virginia. I wonder if his students know that their prof was once a fresh-faced, gold-record rock 'n' roll singer.

Another young entertainer I brought in that year was Ritchie Valens. His smash hit at the time was "Come On, Let's Go." Ritchie played five engagements in and around Vancouver in the winter of '58. Just a few months later, on February 3, 1959, he was killed along with Buddy Holly and J.P. Richardson when their plane crashed in a cornfield in Ames, Iowa.

During that summer, I drove my '57 convertible down to Los Angeles, where radio KFWB really impressed me. It had a star-studded cast, including former Texas deejays Bruce Hayes, Elliott Field and Tom Quillan. Retained from years before were Al Jarvis, Joe Yocam, B. Mitchel Reed and Bill Balance. The ratings for October 1959 reported that 14 of the 19 top-rated deejays were on KFWB. Not a bad statistic.

Program Director Chuck Blore — a facile McLendon protegé from El Paso, Texas — had his own unique theories about rock radio. He said his sole purpose was to have his disc jockeys entertain. "KFWB jocks don't just ad lib...their routines were ultimately scripted, and they were trained to a razor-sharp finesse to make every split second count effectively."

I decided to explore the opportunities in the States. My friend Gil Henry, who had been an inspiration to me earlier when he beamed up to Vancouver from KING Radio in Seattle, was working at KNX doing a West Coast network show on CBS Radio called "The Regal Turntable Show," sponsored by Regal Beer. Gil was good, but rock 'n' roll radio had beaten him. George Jay, a record promoter, and Norm Pringle, a guy I knew from Victoria, B.C., helped me. Norm played a transcription of a telethon for me that was to bring about one of Peggy Lee's biggest sellers.

1958

At the time, Norman's job was to tape local programs and transcribe them for Armed Forces radio shows. Peggy Lee had performed "Fever" live on one of these shows and Norm played it for me in his sound studio. I loved it instantly and asked him for a dub of the performance. I took it back to CKWX in Vancouver and played the living daylights out of it. It wasn't long before Capitol Records took note and released it as a single. I still have a tape recording of Peggy's original telethon performance. Naturally, it's a treasure.

Earlier that year, I booked Gene Vincent and Bonnie Guitar into Vancouver's Denman Auditorium. Gene Vincent and the Blue Caps sounded very much like Elvis Presley and the Jordanaires. But there were subtle differences. Gene and his group won a Capitol Record contest in 1956 when the recording company was searching for an "Elvis-type" singer. He arrived in Los Angeles in the spring of 1956 with a song he and his friend, Sheriff Tex Davis, had written, called "Be-Bop-A-Lula," inspired by the comic strip character Little Lulu. That song became a Top 10 national hit and was Gene's first million seller. In 1958, Gene also appeared with Little Richard and Eddie Cochran in the movie *The Girl Can't Help It*.

The Gene Vincent show had an excellent turnout. There was something sinister about Gene Vincent on stage, although in person he was quiet, humble, and pleasant to know. You could say he was the Mick Jagger of his day — except in personality.

With Gene at that Vancouver performance was Bonnie Guitar, who had started her career in Seattle and recorded "Dark Moon" for Dot Records in March 1957. It was an instant smash hit, even though Bonnie initially had strong competition from singer-actress Gale Storm, who had television exposure on the weekly sitcom "My Little Margie" to help her. Bonnie's next hit was "Mister Fire Eyes." She was one of the very few female singers to have a hit rock 'n' roll record back then and she had great stage presence.

As the pictures in this chapter suggest, 1958 was an extraordinary year for me personally. It was not an exceptional year for rock 'n' roll, however, although there was an interesting mix that year, from Elvis and Gene Vincent and the Champs to Dean Martin, Louis Prima, Keely Smith and Henry Mancini.

But 1959 would prove even more interesting.

Top Ten Hits

1. *Battle of New Orleans* — Johnny Horton
2. *Mack the Knife* — Bobby Darin
3. *Personality* — Lloyd Price
4. *Venus* — Frankie Avalon
5. *Lonely Boy* — Paul Anka
6. *Dream Lover* — Bobby Darin
7. *The Three Bells* — The Browns
8. *Come Softly to Me* — The Fleetwoods
9. *Kansas City* — Wilbert Harrison
10. *Mr. Blue* — The Fleetwoods

On Broadway

A Majority of One
Sweet Bird of Youth
Gypsy
The Sound of Music
Once upon a Mattress
A Raisin in the Sun
Destry Rides Again

Grammy Awards

Record of the Year — *"Mack the Knife"* (Bobby Darin)
Album of the Year — *"Come Dance with Me"* (Frank Sinatra)
Song of the Year — *"Mack the Knife"* (Bobby Darin)
Best Male Vocalist — *Frank Sinatra* ("Come Dance with Me")
Best Female Vocalist — *Ella Fitzgerald* ("But Not for Me")
Best Vocal Group — *Mormon Tabernacle Choir* ("Battle Hymn of the Republic")

On Television

The Untouchables
Bonanza
Dick Clark
Roller Derby
Dobie Gillis

Top Movies

Ben Hur
Anatomy of a Murder
The Diary of Anne Frank
The Nun's Story
Room at the Top
Some Like It Hot
Suddenly Last Summer
Black Orpheus
Porgy and Bess
A Hole in the Wall

The Oscars

Best Picture	*Ben-Hur*
Best Director	William Wyler *(Ben-Hur)*
Best Actor	Charleton Heston *(Ben-Hur)*
Best Actress	Simone Signoret *(Room at the Top)*
Best Supporting Actor	Hugh Griffith *(Ben-Hur)*
Best Supporting Actress	Shelley Winters *(The Diary of Anne Frank)*
Best Song	"High Hopes" by James Van Heusen and Sammy Cahn from *A Hole in the Head*

Best Sellers

From the Terrace
    John O'Hara

Hawaii
    James Michener

The Ugly American
    William J. Lederer and Eugene Burdick

Act One
    Moss Hart

The Status Seekers
    Vance Packard

My Brother Was an Only Child
    Jack Douglas

Twixt Twelve and Twenty
    Pat Boone

Bobby Darin at KGW Radio, Portland, 1959.

Don Gibson and Ferlin Husky back the "Country America Show" on July 1, 1959.

On remote from the makeshift drag strip at the Abbotsford Airport

Broadcasting live at DGWTV in Portland Oregon.

Bill Davis (left), morning man at CKWX, with enfante terrible Red Robinson, in costume

1959

In 1959, young rock 'n' roll stars were becoming involved in the business side of entertainment. Although entertainers have always been notoriously ill informed about the business of show biz, they now began paying attention to it.

Rock 'n' roll was instrumental in bringing about this change. It had ballooned from a pulsating new dance beat into a billion-dollar business. Today some of the richest entertainers, songwriters, and producers in the world make their millions through rock 'n' roll and its numerous related sidelines, including personal appearances, TV shows, movies, T-shirts, and books. The records are the bread and butter — everything else is profit.

On New Year's Eve 1958, I launched a record called "Pink Shoe Laces" by Dodie Stevens, who had been brought to Vancouver by Carl Burns, the owner of her record company, Crystalette. I played the record a couple of times, and it got a terrific response. I never did figure out whether it was because the song was good or because there were so many people listening to CKWX that New Year's Eve.

"Pink Shoe Laces" went on to become a million seller, and Carl Burns informed me that I received official credit for launching the hit. I mention this because in those days a deejay could, at his discretion, air just about anything. Today this freedom is gone. Everything is computerized and systematically tried in larger markets; the human element is missing.

Elvis was in the army in 1959. Even though his records were being released at regular intervals, he failed to dominate the top of the charts and didn't even reach the Top 10. His songs appeared from number 30 on down and included "A Big Hunk of Love," "A Fool Such as I," and "I Need Your Love Tonight," which came in at a lowly 59.

A group called the Crests recorded "Sixteen Candles" in 1959. It was their only million seller. This record came into the spotlight when it was charged in the U.S. Congress, that "American Bandstand" host Dick Clark had played the record only four times in 10 weeks — until, it was reported, he became one of the owners of the record. Then he played it 27 times in less than three months and it took off like a rocket.

Having an ownership in something was dicey then and represents a conflict of interest now. Paying for a play was not new,

1959

however. This practice occurred in the vaudeville days when music publishers gave nonreturnable cash advances for on-stage performances of their songs. Even people like Al Jolson were cut in on songwriting royalties in return for performing particular numbers.

The famous Van Doren TV Quiz Scandal had authorities watching the thriving record business much more carefully than before. Many deejays had been operating a "payola" system, telling the record reps to give them money and they would play their record. Licensed radio station owners in the United States and Canada had to take action instantly against all their on-the-air employees. Each signed a notarized affidavit swearing he had not taken and would not take payola. It was either that or risk the loss of the station's license, which represented no small investment.

The respectability of rock 'n' roll had never been high, but it reached rock bottom when this occurred. Nevertheless, people kept buying records and during 1959 Canadians and Americans increased their record purchases by 20 percent.

There were dozens of articles in newspapers across North America about payola. Aside from anything else, newspaper advertising was getting a good run for its money from the radio stations by this time.

Vancouver Sun staff reporter Bruce Young phoned me in Portland to ask for a quote on the topic and I simply said that Vancouver was not important enough to worry about that scandal. He quoted me that way. But the *Sun* ran the story on page one with a picture of me and a smaller headline saying, "Red Robinson turns back bribes." It was true. In Vancouver, no one had ever approached me, but in Portland a few companies had. I turned them down, not because of my high morals, but because I felt that there's always a hitch with anything "free." In any case, not every deejay was involved in payola and I certainly don't want to suggest that.

Because he was the granddaddy of rock 'n' roll and some thought he looked like a B-movie gangster, Alan Freed was the scapegoat of the payola scandal. Many thought at the time, as I did, that the American congressmen who had investigated the quiz shows were riding high on the publicity they were getting and the payola investigation was an opportunity to stay in the spotlight. Let's face it,

1959

they had discovered the power of radio and television.

Alan Freed was charged with accepting $30,000 in bribes from six record companies. He resigned on the air, crying as he said goodbye to his audience. Then he played "Shimmy, Shimmy, Ko-ko Bop" by Little Anthony and the Imperials. Dozens of other deejays across North America quit under pressure and many more were fired. The point was made and talk about payola died. Alan Freed had been the sacrificial lamb.

In the sixties, the problem of how to reward deejays for their help in making a record a hit was solved by the introduction of "gold" records. These were copies of the actual gold discs awarded to artists for selling a million dollars' worth of singles or albums. The deejays who had helped make the records big would be sent a "gold" copy with their name engraved on the award.

The contribution of deejays has been recognized for decades by the record companies. You can't sell a book if it isn't purchased by the bookstores and you can't sell a record unless it is played by a radio station, featured on TV, made into a movie, or heard at a concert or on Broadway. Deejays today don't have much control over what is played on the air. A music director or librarian selects a list of songs and the announcer or deejay simply plays from the list.

Every once in a while, however, someone does something utterly brilliant and that old payola scandal comes into view again. In 1978 a deejay decided to play Neil Diamond and Barbra Streisand simultaneously, editing together their individual recordings of "You Don't Bring Me Flowers Any More." The result was an immediate hit and the two singers ended up recording the song together and hitting the Top 10 spots across North America.

The record company, Streisand and Diamond were, of course, thrilled and grateful that deejay Gary Guthrie had the imagination to create this production. How to thank him was the problem. Neil and Barbra sent him flowers.

Enough on payola. But more on radio. In 1952, Lloyd Price had written and recorded "Lawdy Miss Clawdy," which was one of the earliest combination rock 'n' roll-rhythm and blues hits. Lloyd's big hit in 1959, "Personality," resulted from a radio commercial that he had co-written, and it went on to become a million seller.

1959

Mike Stoller and Jerry Lieber crop up over and over again as songwriters of considerable stature during this era. Their hits included "Hound Dog" by Elvis, "Poison Ivy" and "Yakety Yak" by the Coasters, "Black Denim Trousers" by the Cheers and "Kansas City" by Wilbert Harrison.

Jazz singers Dinah Washington and Della Reese both had hits in 1959. "What a Difference a Day Makes" established Dinah as more than her nickname, "Queen of the Blues."

Neil Sedaka was a young RCA recording artist and composer in 1959. That year he wrote "Oh, Carol" and dedicated it to his friend, Carole Klein, whom we know today as Carole King. Her album *Tapestry* is one of the greatest and longest-selling albums in the history of the music business. She and her partner, Jerry Goffin, were a songwriting team in the fifties. One of their best-known songs was "Locomotion," which Little Eva recorded in 1962.

The stream of *Gidget* movies that began to appear in 1959 did not have much to do with rock 'n' roll, but they certainly were a statement of the times. Beach parties, surfing and West Coast fashions were the main components of teenage life, which seems straight-laced by today's standards.

Having received a job offer from KGW radio and TV in Portland, Oregon, I moved to the United States in February 1959, leaving Canada behind for a few years. One of the first acts I helped book into Division Street Corral, Portland's largest dance hall, was Conway Twitty, who was the closest thing to Elvis that North America could come up with. Conway's real name was Harold Jenkins, but, like Gerry Dorsey, who became Englebert Humperdinck, he decided it was better promotion to have an unusual name.

Twitty released a Mercury Records single called "I Need Your Lovin' " in 1957, which was a regional hit. When he recorded "It's Only Make Believe" for MGM Records in 1958 and followed that with some other stompers, he became an international hitmaker.

Another act I booked in Portland was Gene Vincent, but his magic of earlier days seemed to be gone. He performed adequately, but his heart was not in it.

Some of the other singers I brought to Portland included Carl Dobkins, Jr. ("If You Don't Want My Lovin'," "Lucky Devil," and

Meeting Johnny Cash for the first time in 1959, Portland.

Backstage with Marty Robbins at the Country America Show, Portland, 1959.

Interviewing Don (middle) and Phil (right) Everly in 1959.

Interviewing Ricky Nelson, Portland, 1959.

1959

"Exclusively Yours"), Bobby Freeman ("Betty Lou's Got a New Pair of Shoes," "I Do the Shimmy-Shimmy," "Do You Want to Dance?" and a 1964 hit, "C'mon and Swim"), Jimmy Clanton ("Just a Dream," "A Letter to an Angel," and "Go Jimmy Go"), and the Frantics, who never really made it on a national scale. They were part of Bob Reisdorf's Dophin Records, which later became Dolton Records.

Reisdorf put together a group called the Fleetwoods, (the name came from the Fleetwood Telephone Exchange in Washington State), who had been students at Olympia High in Washington and wrote the smash number-one 1959 hit, "Come Softly to Me." Reisdorf was also responsible for advancing the career of Vic Dana and the incomparable Ventures. Their first hit, "Walk, Don't Run," was released in June 1959. Reisdorf also helped draw attention to the Pacific Northwest as a source of talent.

The Colony Club in Seattle used to be a well-known spotting ground for future stars. Many established stars also appeared at this club, as they did in Vancouver's Arctic Club and, later, the Cave Supper Club, which the late Ken Stauffer made into a pre-Las Vegas testing stage. Appearing at the Colony one night was a group of fraternity brothers whose harmony later impressed jazz great Dave Brubeck when they appeared at The Hungry i in San Francisco. Brubeck signed the Brothers Four to a Columbia contract. They recorded "Greenfields" in 1959 and this folk ballad by Terry Gilkyson became their first hit.

And where are the Brothers Four now? They toured Japan in 1983, just as *Rockbound* was going to press. Most of the year, original Brothers Four member Dick Foley can be seen daily on KOMO-TV, beamed out of Seattle to Northwest Washington, Oregon and British Columbia.

Another singer spotted at the Colony Club, this time by Bing Crosby, was Pat Suzuki. She later recorded the best-selling Broadway score of "Flower Drum Song."

Down the coast in Portland, everyone remembers the "Prince of Wails" who hails from there, Johnnie Ray. His basket of tearful hits made him one of the most popular artists on the national charts between 1951 and 1956.

1959

I first met Johnny Cash in Portland in 1959. By this time, he was already a legend. He too played the Division Street Corral, so I hauled a tape recorder over there and did my first of several interviews with Johnny. His recording of "I Walk the Line" began a string of hits in 1956 and they haven't stopped coming yet. Today he is not only a giant in the country recording business but also one of the first singers to bridge the gap between country and pop music.

Shortly after Johnny's visit to Portland, I received a telegram from him asking me to help give his new release, "I Got Stripes," and the flip side, "Five Feet High and Rising," a lift. Both "I Got Stripes" and the flip received notice on the national charts (numbers 43 and 76, respectively), but they soared right up the KGW chart in Portland, supporting my theory that personal appearances will blow up a record. Over the years, I have spent many hours with Johnny and consider him a friend. Most recently, I emceed his performance during his 1976 tour of North American fairs.

As 1959 drew to a close, the weekly Hit Parade charts sported quite a mixture. From Marty Robbins singing one of his greatest hits, "El Paso," to Freddy Cannon's "Way Down Yonder in New Orleans," Paul Anka's wailing of "It's Time to Cry," Bobby Darin's "Mack the Knife" and Steve Lawrence's "Pretty Blue Eyes," the music was a potpourri of styles and themes.

This would be the last year for "Your Hit Parade" and the 30-year-old "Voice of Firestone," a long-standing radio show. Nineteen fifty-nine was also one of the final years of youthful innocence.

Top Ten Hits

1. *Theme from a Summer Place* — Percy Faith
2. *He'll Have to Go* — Jim Reeves
3. *Cathy's Clown* — The Everly Brothers
4. *Running Bear* — Johnny Preston
5. *Teen Angel* — Mark Dinning
6. *It's Now or Never* — Elvis Presley
7. *Handy Man* — Jimmy Jones
8. *I'm Sorry* — Brenda Lee
9. *Stuck on You* — Elvis Presley
10. *The Twist* — Chubby Checker

Grammy Awards

Record of the Year — *"Theme from a Summer Place"* (Percy Faith)
Album of the Year — *Button Down Mind* (Bob Newhart)
Song of the Year — *"Theme from Exodus"* (Ernest Gold)
Best Male Vocalist — *Ray Charles* ("Georgia on My Mind")
Best Female Vocalist — *Ella Fitzgerald* ("Mack the Knife")
Best Vocal Group — *Steve Lawrence and Eydie Gorme* ("We Got Us")

On Broadway

A Thurber Carnival
Bye, Bye, Birdie
West Side Story
Camelot
A Taste of Honey
The Fantasticks
Do Re Mi

Top Movies

The Apartment
The Alamo
Elmer Gantry
Sons and Lovers
The Sundowners
Journey to the Center of the Earth
Never on Sunday
Psycho
Butterfield 8
Exodus
G.I. Blues

On Television

Jackie Gleason
Dinah Shore
Candid Camera
Peter Gunn
Hawaiian Eye

Best Sellers

The Leopard
   Guiseppe de Lampedisa

To Kill a Mockingbird
   Harper Lee (Pulitzer Prize winner, 1961)

The Rise and Fall of the Third Reich
   William L. Shirer

Born Free
   Joy Adamson

The Waste Makers
   Vance Packard

The Oscars

Best Picture	*The Apartment*
Best Director	Billy Wilder *(The Apartment)*
Best Actor	Burt Lancaster *(Elmer Gantry)*
Best Actress	Elizabeth Taylor *(Butterfield 8)*
Best Supporting Actor	Peter Ustinov *(Spartacus)*
Best Supporting Actress	Shirley Jones *(Elmer Gantry)*
Best Song	"Never on Sunday" by Manos Hadjidakis from *Never on Sunday*

1960

Another opening, another show. That's how I view the start of the sixties and a new decade. We didn't know it at the time, but by the middle of the decade there would be a complete change and the world would be a different place. The music world would be rocked by an unforgettable phenomenon — the Beatles.

The 1960 Oregon Primary Campaign was in full swing as I did my daily stint at KGW Radio in Portland. As a result, I got to meet then-Senator John F. Kennedy and Vice-President Richard Nixon. In addition, I met a handful of entertainers, including Don Gibson and the Everly Brothers, as they swung through the Pacific Northwest on their various tours.

The biggest event of the year for rock 'n' roll was the return of Elvis Presley from the army. The most beloved GI in the world hadn't conquered any countries, but he had maintained his massive following of fans. As more people heard his records and saw his movies, Elvis Presley continued to dominate the rock 'n' roll scene, even though he wouldn't dominate the highly competitive radio hit charts again.

While Elvis was in the army, the "plastic rockers" had taken top spots on the nation's radio playlists. We called them "plastic rockers" because they never would be the original Elvis Presley. They were copies, some of them good, but most second rate, trying to fill the void Elvis left when he joined the army.

Headquarters for this company of replacements continued to be the Philadelphia-originated "American Bandstand" TV program, which was still a showplace for newcomers. Glamor, fame and wealth were fleeting for many who appeared on the show, but some, such as Fabian, Frankie Avalon, Paul Anka, Dion, the Fleetwoods and Connie Francis, had longer careers. Connie Francis was one of the few female rock 'n' roll stars of any consequence until Diana Ross and the Supremes came along and until Cher began to take off with Sonny.

In 1960, Frank Sinatra, who has always supported young talent, paid Elvis a huge sum to appear on his TV program. At the time, Frank was an aging 44 years old. Who could have imagined that he would continue to be a superstar for at least another 20 years? Elvis was just 25 years old, full of youth and energy — the epitome of success.

1960

On television, appearing before a live audience at the Fountainbleau Hotel in Miami Beach, they represented the music idols of two generations. Elvis was the model of a modern star. His sideburns were gone and the cameras did not have to monitor his movements below the waist. He even wore a tuxedo at one point in the show. Although Elvis was still the ultimate male sex symbol, the jerks and sexy moves were gone. The Elvis of 1960 was an adult with infinitely more sophistication than before.

His appearance with Frank Sinatra gave evidence of his enduring popularity. The TV show was a landmark. Millions watched excitedly as Elvis introduced his new single, "Stuck on You," with "Fame and Fortune" as the flip side. The pinnacle of the evening, however, was when Elvis sang Frank's hit "Witchcraft" and Frank sang Elvis's hit "Love Me Tender" — it was a magic moment. The girls in the audience screamed and the people at home were thrilled. Elvis had not lost his magic. He would go on to become an even bigger legend than he had been before entering the army.

That night, 68 per cent of all television sets across North America were tuned in to watch Elvis. Such an audience was astounding for 1960 and even today it is a remarkable percentage of people watching one show. But it showed that Elvis had returned triumphant and was heralding a major shift in the rock world. The days of "pretty" voices would last only a few years and then the public would rebel. Although no one in North America knew anything about them yet, the Beatles were already performing in Germany.

Collectors agree that the first Elvis album after his return from the army, *Elvis Is Back*, was his best. It contains some of the best rhythm and blues numbers he ever performed and you'll even find Elvis camping it up, warbling and generally expressing his capricious personality with strange noises and sound effects.

Elvis starred in two movies upon his return, *G.I. Blues*, which was one of his most successful movies, and *Flaming Star*. Presley fans were not in the least amused with *Flaming Star*. Director Don Siegal insisted that Elvis not sing during this movie, so he hummed along to the tune of "A Cane and High Starch Collar." This film was a huge disappointment to his millions of fans.

To imply that Elvis was the only show in America that year

Bob Reisdorf, president of Dolton Records, introduced Bonnie Guitar, Vic Dana, the Ventures, and the Fleetwoods. In this 1960 photo, he introduces the Frantics (three middle) to me at KGW, Portland.

With Bob Luman and Buddy Clyde at the Queen Elizabeth Theatre

"Doing my stint for the U.S. Army."

I was not a drag-stripper, but my Ford convertible was customized.

1960

would be misleading. There was a lot going on, but not much in rock 'n' roll was memorable.

A raft of teenage movies emerged from Hollywood as producers and directors tried desperately to revive interest in movies. Mickey Rooney, the oldest child on earth, played a divorced father seeking facts about his dead son in a melodrama called *Platinum High School*, which also starred Terry Moore, Dan Duryea and Sal Mineo (a true rock 'n' roll movie hero who dressed and acted the part) and introduced Conway Twitty, who sang the title song of the movie. Canada's own Paul Anka (how he must hate that title today!) sang "Ave Marie" and "Lonely Boy" in *Platinum High School*, so all was not entirely lost. Maybe she was trying to prove that blondes can have more fun and get away with it, but Mamie Van Doren's portrayal of a rebel leader in this second-rate movie (and I'm being generous) was notable for one reason — it was the first time a star was seen chewing gum with her mouth open.

Because They're Young may play on the late, late show, or as a Saturday afternoon filler on occasion, but I haven't noticed it for years. Yes, that was Dick Clark of "American Bandstand" playing the role of a teacher in the movie, which also starred Tuesday Weld, Doug McClure and Bobby Rydell. Bobby sang "Swinging School," which rose to number five on the U.S. pop charts. The title song of the movie was sung by Jimmy Darren. Duane Eddy and the Rebel Rousers also appeared in the movie. Now, if you ever appear on a "trivia" program, you'll know some of the least important facts ever asked for.

Out of Tacoma, Washington, came a four-piece band called the Ventures, who recorded "Walk, Don't Run," a real rocker that would pave the way for many local rock bands. The Ventures walked into a recording studio, bought time, and recorded their instrumental. That was the beginning of the independent production house that is prevalent in the business today.

Rock 'n' roll lost two stars in 1960. A taxi crash in London killed Eddie Cochran and hospitalized Gene Vincent. Johnny Horton, who recorded "Battle of New Orleans" and "Sink the Bismark" to great success, was enroute to Nashville when the car in which he was riding crashed. He had been Johnny Cash's closest friend. Everyone felt the loss.

1960

Country writer-singer Johnny Tillotson from Jacksonville, Florida, came out with "Poetry in Motion" in 1960, and young Chubby Checker was singing songs about the twist. While the songs were popular, the actual dance didn't really catch on for another year.

Percy Faith, a conductor-arranger and composer from Winnipeg, Manitoba, struck it rich with the "Theme from a Summer Place" in 1960, while Jack Scott of Windsor, Ontario, was burning a few bridges with his hit, "What in the World Has Come Over You." Along with Paul Anka, these artists gave credibility to the Canadian music industry, which, until the late sixties and seventies, didn't make much of a mark on pop music.

Novelty songs took off and "Alley Oop," based on the cartoon strip, scored a victory for the Hollywood Argyles. And who can forget "Itsy Bitsy Teenie Weenie Yellow Polka Dot Bikini," which propelled Brian Hyland to number 19 on the year's best-seller chart?

Sometimes I catch a rerun of "The Bob Newhart Show," or see Bob in a TV interview or on another show and am amazed at his durability. In 1960, Bob was a very popular comic who had two of the top five best-selling albums, *The Buttoned Down Mind of Bob Newhart* and *The Buttoned Down Mind Strikes Back*. Another example of early sixties humor was Shelly Berman, who could convulse a house party with his much-played comedy albums. But the big seller was the *Sound of Music* sound track LP from the Broadway musical, which went on to become an all-time Hollywood blockbuster.

Part of being young and a resident of the United States in the fifties and sixties was automatic service in the U.S. Armed Forces. In February, 1960, I became Robert G. Robinson, attached to the Oregon National Guard.

I was later shipped to Fort Ord, California. It was there that I met entertainer Bobby Bare, whose hit was "All American Boy." The record was credited to Bill Parsons — one of the reasons why Bobby moved on to other labels, among them Valient, Fraternity and RCA.

Meeting Bobby Darin at the Oregon Centennial Exposition was another exciting moment for me in 1960. Bobby was in one of his many transitional periods. By that I mean he was trying to change his image from "Splash Splash" rock 'n' roll writer, composer and

1960

performer to middle-of-the-road entertainer, a new-generation Frank Sinatra. Bobby was forever looking for an identity and his search never ended. It was at this time that he introduced the KGW TV and radio audience to his new album, *That's All*, which included the classic "Mack the Knife."

When you meet and interview entertainers you naturally form your own opinion of them. In person, I found Bobby Darin very interesting, but he was always trying to prove himself smarter than you. Some found his one-upmanship disagreeable. Once you understood Darin and his insecurity, however, you understood the man who was a fine songwriter and an outstanding showman and musician. His death of heart failure cut short what would have been a brilliant career.

Like most rock 'n' roll deejays then and now, I had the habit of turning up the monitors so that the volume was enough to drive a herd of elephants wild. So KGW Program Director Don Porter asked me to keep it down, as there was a Senator Kennedy coming in to do some taping.

John F. Kennedy was in and out of KGW Radio that fall during the Oregon Primary taping public service announcements for various health and charity organizations. We met after one of these sessions and he thanked me for keeping the "pounding sound" at a reasonable level. We spoke then and later when he was at the station. I remember that he impressed me, but because I was a Canadian living in the United States and was not interested in politics at that time, I didn't really know who this senator was.

I also met Richard Nixon in the lobby of KGW Radio and Television. I saw the vice-presidential limousine outside the door, walked out to have a look at it and was grabbed by two security guards who took me back into the lobby and verified that I was, indeed, a deejay and an employee at the station. They apologized, explained the importance of security and offered to introduce me to the vice-president.

Richard Nixon came down the stairs from the TV studio and was quickly introduced to a group of us. My impressions were that he lacked warmth and was a much bigger man than one would gather from his photographs and TV appearances.

1960

These are the brushes with history that deejays had in the fifties and sixties and sometimes in the seventies. Today, unless you are a hotliner or a news person, you simply don't meet the VIPs — whether they're politicians, film stars, or recording stars. They are all protected and isolated from the populace and much of the media.

At the end of 1960, we were on a crest. Elvis was back in the picture, President Kennedy was about to be inaugurated and the youth movement was going strong.

Top Ten Hits

1. Tossin' and Turnin' — Bobby Lewis
2. It's Gonna Work Out Fine — Ike and Tina Turner
3. Don't Cry No More — Bobby Bland
4. Hide Away — Freddy King
5. Shop Around — The Miracles
6. My True Story — The Jive Five
7. I Like It Like That — Chris Kenner
8. Stand by Me — Ben E. King
9. Mother-in-Law — Ernie K-Doe
10. All in My Mind — Maxine Brown

Grammy Awards

Record of the Year — *"Moon River"* (Henry Mancini)
Album of the Year — *"Judy at Carnegie Hall"* (Judy Garland)
Song of the Year — *"Moon River"* (Henry Mancini and Johnny Mercer)
Best Male Vocalist — *Jack Jones* ("Lollipops and Roses")
Best Female Vocalist — *Judy Garland* ("Judy at Carnegie Hall")
Best Vocal Group — *Lambert, Hendrick, and Ross* ("High Flying")

On Broadway

Come Blow Your Horn
A Shot in the Dark
Take Her, She's Mine
Milk and Honey
Subways Are for Sleeping
How to Succeed in Business without Really Trying

On Television

Dr. Kildare
Surfside 6
Danny Thomas

Top Movies

West Side Story
Fanny
The Guns of Navarone
The Hustler
La Dolce Vita
Breakfast at Tiffany's
Splendor in the Grass
Pocketful of Miracles
Flower Drum Song
The World of Susie Wong

The Oscars

Best Picture	*West Side Story*
Best Director	Jerome Robbins, Robert Wise *(West Side Story)*
Best Actor	Maximilian Schell *(Judgment at Nuremberg)*
Best Actress	Sophia Loren *(Two Women)*
Best Supporting Actor	George Chakiris *(West Side Story)*
Best Supporting Actress	Rita Moreno *(West Side Story)*
Best Song	"*Moon River*" by Henry Mancini and Johnny Mercer from *Breakfast at Tiffany's*

Best Sellers

The Carpetbaggers
   Harold Robbins

Franny and Zooey
   J. D. Salinger

The Incredible Journey
   Sheila Bumford

To Kill a Mockingbird
   Harper Lee

Before I Sleep
   Thomas A. Dooley
Living Free
   Joy Adamson

1961

At the beginning of 1961, the world watched through the window of television as John F. Kennedy was inaugurated President of the United States of America. The age of Camelot was upon us.

Never before had an American president and his wife had such impact on the youth of America. Kennedy's youthful appearance, idealistic philosophy and powerful media presence inspired the confidence of Americans — and the rest of the world. While not all of us agreed with all of his political theories, we were interested in what he had to say. We had found a hero. For the first time, North American teenagers took an active role in politics. This same type of charismatic leader surfaced in Canada when Pierre Elliott Trudeau amazed political pundits and emerged as Canada's youthful prime minister in 1968.

Media attention focused on the White House like a giant strobe light. The press reported every detail of Jackie Kennedy's hats, bouffant hair style, designer clothes, Porthault sheets and even her size 10 feet perched on small stacked heels. The president's flamboyant personal life and the Kennedys' jet-set style of entertaining brought a new elegance to the White House that was copied by many — including those on beer budgets with blue-collar ambitions.

Twenty years later, Lady Diana Spencer created a similar furor when she married Prince Charles. Lady Di hair styles and fashions became the rage. Until Jackie Kennedy appeared, however, elegance, and high fashion had been absent from North American life. We still had a frugal attitude, left over from the Second World War.

In 1961, rock 'n' roll had an irrevocable place on radio stations across North America. In fact, the rock revolt was taking hold around the world. It had penetrated even the most prestigious radio playlists. We were considered "bad boys" because we played rock 'n' roll — yet this was the kind of radio that sold — and sold well. Stodgy advertising agencies were horrified when they realized that if they wanted to sell their products, they were going to have to buy time on rock 'n' roll programs. Parents continued to worry that rock 'n' roll music would have a bad influence on their children. Within a few years, however, the new set of young parents would be graduates of the Bill Haley and Elvis Presley school of rock, and they would be

1961

playing rock 'n' roll themselves. As Sonny Bono sang a few years later, the beat goes on.

In looking over the charts of 1961 and replaying some of the hits, you can't help noticing that it was an absolute grab bag of style, content and sound. Chubby Checker emerged as a singer to be reckoned with in "Pony Time" and Gene McDaniels had one of the most memorable numbers of the year with "One Hundred Pounds of Clay."

Del Shannon's "Runaway" not only hit the top of the charts, but it turned out to be one of the biggest sellers of the year. He followed it with "Hats Off to Larry" and became a significant part of the rock picture of the early sixties.

Roy Orbison hit the charts with "Crying" and "Running Scared," a classic. He and Shannon formed the backbone of the influential 1961 group. Orbison first came into the spotlight as one of Elvis Presley's pals who started recording at the old Sun studios. "Rock House" and "Oobie Doobie" were two songs that Orbison wrote and performed. When he teamed up with Joe Melson, Orbison's songwriting abilities brought him to the forefront, where he remains today, over 20 years later.

Bobby Vee was one of the group of Bobbys who surfaced in the early sixties. (Remember Bobby Curtola, Bobby Vinton, Bobby Bare and, later, Bobbie Gentry?) What was unusual about Bobby Vee was his historic relationship to Buddy Holly. Vee was the young lad who filled in at the last minute for Buddy Holly at the tragic concert in February 1959 at Fargo, North Dakota. Don McLean would later write about it as the concert that didn't take place. By this time, however, he was a top-selling artist in his own right. His style was very much like Buddy Holly's style, and he also recorded on Liberty Records. At one time he went on tour and recorded as Bobby Vee and the Crickets — yes, it was the same group that Buddy Holly had formed. That did not last long, however. Bobby had a hit in 1970 called "Sweet Sweetheart."

Someone else in the limelight that year was Chris Kenner, who sang the suggestive "I Like It Like That." A real thumper was "Quarter to Three," performed by the U.S. Bonds. Twenty years later Gary U.S. Bond emerged again for a brief recovery on the road in the United States.

Buddy Knox of "Party Doll" fame, 1961.

Backstage with Johnny Cash at the Cave Supper Club, 1961.

With Jim Reeves in Vancouver, 1961. The memory lives on.

Typical dance scene back in 1961, Vancouver.

1961

Singer Neil Sedaka deserves a mention for 1961, although he didn't make the Top 10 that year. Like a lot of musicians and entertainers in those days, he had many regional hits. The reason? Before the large-scale impact of television, radio stations could create their own hits, reflecting the tastes of their local audiences. Today the same tunes are popular in New York, Vancouver, Los Angeles, London and Adelaide. Sedaka did attain success with two songs he had coauthored, "Calendar Girl" and "Happy Birthday, Sweet Sixteen." He also penned "Little Devil" and "Sweet Little You." Neil rolled along for many years with a string of successful hits, including two of my favorites, "Breakin' Up Is Hard to Do," which he first recorded in 1962, and "That's When the Music Takes Me," which was introduced in 1975.

Many musicians fade away after a few years, never to be heard of again and others make remarkable comebacks. Neil Sedaka had been in a slump for several years when he was asked if he would like to work with Elton John. He did and the resulting "Laughter in the Rain" is a timeless tune that propelled him to the top of the charts everywhere.

About the same time, a little-known singing duo had been touring the clubs in California. Both members were very talented — she was Toni Tenille, then a club singer and sometime actress; he was Daryl Dragon, the son of the famous Carmen Dragon of the Hollywood Bowl Symphony. They recorded "Love Will Keep Us Together" as the Captain and Tenille, and it became a runaway hit single and subsequent album. On the album cut, you can hear the phrase "Sedaka is back," which related the Captain and Tenille very nicely to Neil Sedaka and didn't hurt Sedaka's image either. Today Neil continues to thrill crowds in person and on television with his showmanship and his romantic tunes.

Does talent run in the family? Sedaka can often be seen performing with his daughter, Dara, who is also a singer. Other show business offspring from around the same time include Nat "King" Cole's daughter, Natalie Cole, and, of course, Patti Davis, daughter of President Reagan.

Ike and Tina Turner had a hit called "It's Gonna Work Out Fine," which did well everywhere. Their first recording on the charts

1961

was "A Fool in Love," released in 1960. Their last hit together was "Baby Get It On," in 1975. As a team they were terrific, but, as a single act since the seventies, Tina Turner has surpassed the appeal she and Ike enjoyed to become a big-name draw everywhere.

And Elvis? He performed at a benefit in Honolulu for the U.S.S. *Arizona* in 1961 — his last public appearance until 1968.

As far as movies went, there was a sad lack of creative genius in the early sixties. Just take a look at *Where the Boys Are*, which starred Connie Francis. I don't know anybody who really liked the song from the movie, which topped the charts, but it did show that Connie Francis had staying power. The movie was instantly forgettable, but Connie doesn't quit — she is still carrying on like a trouper today.

In 1961, what I would term the first true rock 'n' roll attitudinal musical hit the Great White Way when Leonard Bernstein's *West Side Story* broke all records on Broadway. It showed gangs, peer pressure, racial tension between Puerto Ricans and Italians and the effect of all this on a teenage love affair. Of course, the conflict between Puerto Ricans and Italians mirrored the real-life conflict between WASPs and other ethnic groups, particularly blacks. *West Side Story* was a powerful statement about the problems facing those who didn't fit into the pattern of the majority — a recurring theme in rock 'n' roll music as well.

Once in a while a movie, play, or musical comes along that has a strong message for you personally. One such movie for me was *They Shoot Horses, Don't They?*. This movie came out in the seventies, and the message was: It just isn't worth it to destroy your body for money or fame. Evel Knievel may have made his million that way, but it certainly was not my method.

I really learned this lesson in 1961. As a young deejay, I would try anything to increase my ratings, prove that I was almost indestructible and gain attention. Stunts were fun. So when a group of skydivers and "hard hat" undersea divers asked me to try a double escapade up in the sky and down in the waters of Howe Sound, I decided to try it.

Jimmy Dean had made the Second Narrows Bridge in Vancouver famous with his song "Steel Men," which told how 23 men

Going underwater to broadcast live on CKWX, 1961.

With Johnny Cash on stage at the Queen Elizabeth Theatre in Vancouver.

1961

lost their lives when the bridge collapsed in 1958. There was a lot of controversy about how this tragic event had happened, and the speculation and news stories continued for years.

We practiced for the dive in a 12-meter tank. The underwater diver had arranged for a microphone hookup to the surface in order to broadcast the event. He tried it and the test went off beautifully. Then I donned my costume and was lowered into the murky waters of Howe Sound near the bridge. To experience an old-fashioned "hard hat" dive is almost beyond description. Remember, these were the days before Jacques Cousteau had popularized the new SCUBA apparel and equipment, which is not so heavy and not so dangerous. The contraption that you've seen in dozens of old TV movies is heavy and difficult to maneuver. The show went on, we broadcast live under the water and I decided this would be my last stunt.

Shortly after, I was invited to finish the second part of the two-part challenge: go skydiving. This will bring smiles to everyone who knows me — I'm terrified of air travel. I'll take a train, a bus, a car, a bike, or even walk, but when it comes to air travel, my wife Carol has to hold my hand all the way through the trip. Imagine, if you will, in the days before air travel was as simple as riding on a trolley, my idea of a sky dive. I got as far as suiting up and getting set to jump. But when I looked out of the Cessna 180 window, flying over the Abbotsford airport, I ended the bravado and declined to jump. Maybe I was chicken, but I decided then and there you can only go so far for show business.

I met a number of great people in 1961. One of them was Gene McDaniels. He had the same kind of animal magnetism and professionalism that Lou Rawls had. McDaniels was a charming, intelligent man who had no desire for the notoriety and glory of a rock star. His song "A Hundred Pounds of Clay" was basically a story about God making man and woman from clay. Quite harmless and based on a theme from the Bible. Some people took violent exception to this rock 'n' roll version of creation, however, and it was banned on most commercial radio stations in England and on stations throughout North America. Gene helped bridge the gap between Elvis and the Beatles with such hits as "Tower of Strength," "Chip, Chip," "Point of No Return," "Spanish Lace," and "It's a Lonely Town." These songs were written by some of America's best songwriters, including

1961

Bacharach and David, Goffin and King, and Pomus and Shuman. Today Gene McDaniels is a major American recording producer. But he's still remembered by real rock 'n' rollers for his contribution to the rock of 1961.

I also met Jim Reeves in 1961 when he performed at the Cave Supper Club in Vancouver. When Jim Reeves died in a 1964 plane crash, Charlie Rich saluted him with a song called "Gentleman Jim." A former disc jockey with a powerful baritone voice, Jim Reeves was a gentleman and the ambassador of good will for country music. More than anyone else, except maybe Eddy Arnold, Jim Reeves was able to circumvent the idea that country music was hillbilly music. Like Frank Sinatra, Perry Como and Andy Williams, Jim Reeves made himself a place as a singer of pop country music.

Nearly 20 years later, Jim's ballads continue to be best sellers. His biggest hit was "He'll Have to Go," which broke in early 1960. As early as 1957 he had a solid hit with "Four Walls."

Reeves had also been a baseball player for the St. Louis Cardinals until a leg injury put an end to that career. Then he became a disc jockey for a short time. The guitar remained his first love, however, and he was able to turn his hobby into a full-time career of singing and composing, making him one of the most financially successful country singers of all time.

It is astonishing that Jim's records continue to top the country charts each year — even in the eighties. When I interviewed his wife, Mary, a few years ago, she told me that Jim used to sit down and record a song or two each week at their home studio. He once remarked to Mary: "If anything happens to me, you've got an income for the rest of your life."

After Jim died, his tapes began to be released at regular intervals and they continue to be released today. Mary is a clever business woman. To this day, millions of people enjoy Jim Reeves music without realizing that he died in 1964.

To sum up 1961, I would say that it was basically a boring year. We did a lot of promotion around the records that were released, but it was a quiet, comfortable year. The age of Camelot had another effect — it lulled us into complacency between revolutions. Musically, the world was waiting for the Beatles to recreate an excitement that had not existed since Elvis Presley burst onto the scene in 1955.

1962

On Broadway

Mary, Mary
Carnival
I Can Get It for You Wholesale
A Man for All Seasons
The Night of the Iguana

Top Ten Hits

1. *Stranger on the Shore* — Acker Bilk
2. *I Can't Stop Loving You* — Ray Charles
3. *Mashed Potato Time* — Dee Dee Sharp
4. *Roses Are Red* — Bobby Vinton
5. *The Stripper* — David Rose
6. *Johnny Angel* — Shelly Fabares
7. *The Loco-Motion* — Little Eva
8. *Let Me In* — The Sensations
9. *The Twist* — Chubby Checker
10. *Soldier Boy* — The Shirelles

Grammy Awards

Record of the Year	"I Left My Heart in San Francisco" (Tony Bennett)
Album of the Year	"The First Family" (Vaughan Meader)
Song of the Year	"What Kind of Fool Am I?" (Leslie Bricusse and Anthony Newley)
Best Male Vocalist	*Tony Bennett* ("I Left My Heart in San Francisco")
Best Female Vocalist	*Ella Fitzgerald* ("Ella Swings Brightly with Nelson Riddle")
Best Vocal Group	*Peter, Paul and Mary* ("If I Had a Hammer")

Top Movies

Lawrence of Arabia
The Longest Day
Mutiny on the Bounty
What Ever Happened to Baby Jane?
The Manchurian Candidate
Lolita
The Miracle Worker
Gypsy
The Days of Wine and Roses
Bird Man of Alcatraz
The Music Man

Best Sellers

The Reivers
  William Faulkner

Ship of Fools
  Katherine Anne Porter

Dearly Beloved
  Anne Morrow Lindbergh

Youngblood Hawk
  Herman Wouk

Shade of Difference
  Alan Drury

Calories Don't Count
  Herman Taller

On Television

Bonanza
The Lucy Show
The Danny Thomas Show
Walt Disney
Lassie
Peter Gunn
Maverick
The Tonight Show with Johnny Carson
The Virginian
Wagon Train

The Oscars

Best Picture	*Lawrence of Arabia*
Best Director	David Lean *(Lawrence of Arabia)*
Best Actor	Gregory Peck *(To Kill a Mockingbird)*
Best Actress	Anne Bancroft *(The Miracle Worker)*
Best Supporting Actor	Ed Begley *(Sweet Bird of Youth)*
Best Supporting Actress	Patty Duke *(The Miracle Worker)*
Best Song	"The Days of Wine and Roses" by Henry Mancini and Johnny Mercer from *The Days of Wine and Roses*

1962

The shake and rattle had been drummed out of rock 'n' roll. By 1962 it appeared that rock 'n' roll was in a holding pattern for future revival. Some thought rock 'n' roll and its related fads were dead. Although Elvis Presley's album *Blue Hawaii* was a top seller, and continues to be today, Elvis was not dominating the Top 10 chart. His renditions of "Can't Help Falling in Love," "Return to Sender" and "Good Luck Charm" were in the Top 50, but you couldn't say that Elvis was the main motivator in 1962.

That British band leader Acker Bilk should have the number one best-selling song in North America is a clear sign that we were sitting around, like strangers on the shore, waiting for a new tide to roll in. "Stranger on the Shore" was a pretty instrumental ballad, typifying what "trad" music was all about. The popularity of this song was also an early sign that the British were coming.

Other traditional songs that were popular included the instrumental "Midnight in Moscow," which put Kenny Ball in the limelight for awhile, "The Stripper" by David Rose and his Orchestra, and "Petite Fleur" with Chris Barber, which brought a little musical happiness and fantasy to suburbia.

Neil Sedaka's "Breakin' Up Is Hard to Do" captured the number 15 spot for 1962. Claude King scored for country music with "Wolverton Mountain" at number 16, followed by Chubby Checker at number 17 with "Slow Twistin'," a successor to "The Twist." Joey Dee and the Starlighters put New York's Peppermint Lounge on the map with "The Peppermint Twist."

Even Sam Cooke had a song about the twist, "Twistin' the Night Away." The twist was terrific exercise, but it signaled the end of ballroom or "touch" dancing. From that point on, the dances that were popularized on "American Bandstand" and improvised at high school dances became the thing to do. If you didn't learn them, you looked like someone from the sticks on the dance floor.

Just as energetically, the Isley Brothers sang "Twist and Shout" and Chubby Checker retained yet another position on the hit parade with "Limbo Rock," adding a Caribbean calypso flavor to this new fad — and delighting calypso fans of the fifties who had grown up singing and dancing to the pop calypso sounds of Harry Belafonte.

Folk music had always been popular, and at every college

1962

and university people sat around and sang songs for entertainment. Now folk songs began creeping onto the Hit Parade.

Television networks, at that time forever on the trail of what was popular, began featuring all sorts of programs with "hootenanny" in the title — none of which were all that popular. Radio followed, of course, trying to cash in on this 1962 buzzword. You might say that the folk music and hootenanny craze replaced the calypso fad of the fifties. Neither musical form would make a strong statement in comparison to rock 'n' roll.

In 1962 Curtis Lee had written "Pretty Little Angel Eyes," which was not a giant success in New York, so he returned to his hometown of Hollywood and eventually formed a quartet of black female singers called the Crystals. They recorded a song by Gene Pitney called "He's a Rebel," which was number 50 for the year.

Meanwhile, Gerry Goffin and Carole King had written "The Loco-Motion," which Little Eva made popular, and were subsequently asked to write a hit for the Drifters. The result was "Up on the Roof." Gerry and Carole were an incredibly talented team, and Carole went on to a successful solo career in the seventies, when her own recordings took off.

Surfing had been popular in California and Hawaii for many years, but in 1962 the rest of the world caught on to this sport through the music of the Beach Boys. Their first record, "Surfin'," was a hit only in California, but they followed it up with a national hit called "Surfin' Safari," which floated them to the attention of everyone who ever imagined riding the crest of a huge wave.

From Brazil came the bossa nova and a batch of jazz-folk music that ended up on the pop parades and kept the Arthur Murray Dance Studios busy as people flocked to learn the new dances. Whether it was twisting, surf-twisting on the beach, doing the bossa nova, or enjoying old-time music, people were dancing again.

Bruce Channel had a million seller in 1962 called "Hey, Baby." Like Elvis, he was a graduate of the "Louisiana Hayride Country Show" in the late fifties and early sixties. This song came back in 1982 as a big hit for Anne Murray.

A young Canadian, Bobby Curtola, had an international hit with "Fortune Teller." He had ambitious management and did many

Rosemary Clooney at the Cave, 1962.

Taping an interview with Pearl Bailey, Vancouver, 1962.

Peggy (Keenan) Hodgins interviews Harry Belafonte, Toronto, 1962.

My prized photo of Louis "Satchmo" Armstrong, Vancouver, 1962.

1962

radio station promotions across Canada that year. He was fun to work with because he was enthusiastic, and if his voice wasn't as developed as it should have been, his attitude and personality made up for it.

The music world turned full circle in 1962 when Ray Charles did a reversal of the cover record. After all those years of white singers putting out their sanitized versions of black rhythm and blues hits, Ray Charles scored with an album of white country blues. The hottest single hit from the album became a multimillion seller — Don Gibson's "I Can't Stop Loving You." Ray added his soul sound to the country words, and it was magic. Ray's country blues ran up the pop charts as well as the rhythm and blues charts, and for the first time a black man's music was on the country charts. It was a turning point in the history of American music. At last, total integration was here. Elvis and others began the process in 1954 and Ray Charles completed it in 1962.

Some stars have a larger-than-life image they can't possibly live up to. Others somehow manage to be as great as their image. One such entertainer — a superstar whose popularity continues to build each year — is Pat Boone. Since I first met Pat in 1962, I have grown to admire the man through countless interviews and, in later years, through our work together on various shows, including the annual Timmy Telethon, which is a 24-hour broadcast soliciting funds for the B.C. Lions Society for Crippled Children.

Pat Boone was one of the first white singers to "cover" the black rock 'n' roll records of the fifties. "Ain't That a Shame" had been aired on the black stations throughout North America and was a powerful hit for Fats Domino. Then along came Boone — who traces his ancestry back to the Daniel Boone of American history and folklore — singing this song for white audiences. It proved to be the launching pad for his career.

There is the "odd" critic (and you can read in that anything you wish) who has become upset over the popularity of cover records — especially in the fifties and early sixties. There were those who claimed that Fats Domino and Little Richard were the originals and that Pat Boone's renditions of their hits weren't valid. I disagree. Understand one thing: some people may never have had the chance to hear and enjoy those songs and later to hear them sung by black

1962

innovators who deserve the credit had it not been for singers willing to take a chance — singers like Pat Boone and the McGuire Sisters.

I first met Pat in 1962, but back in 1957, during my Elvis Presley marathon interview, Elvis told me he thought that Pat Boone was one of the finest singers around. Quite an accolade. But then, Pat Boone's quite a guy!

Back in the fifties and sixties, a clean-cut, all American College graduate (wearing those infamous white buck shoes) singing earthy rock 'n' roll was by far the exception and not the rule. Pat Boone most assuredly did not fit into the Elvis, Gene Vincent, Chuck Berry style — especially not the macho style of James Dean and Marlon Brando, who were captivating the newly named teenagers. It was Boone's boyish good looks and charm that made rock 'n' roll acceptable to the white adult audience of the fifties. (What parent could object to rock 'n' roll if it was performed by Pat Boone?)

Riding the crest with Moody River and Speedy Gonzales in 1962, Boone's list of hits are completely diverse, including "April Love," "Tuiti Fruiti," "Love Letters in the Sand," "Ain't That a Shame," "At My Front Door," Tra La La La," "Bernardine" and "Exodus" (for which he wrote the lyrics).

Trivia and nostalgia buffs might want to know that Pat Boone was born in Nashville, Tennessee, in 1934, where he later met and married his wife Shirley, the daughter of western star Red Foley. Before "Ain't That a Shame" blasted onto the charts, he had an earlier recording on Republic, "Until You Tell Me So," and later signed with Dot. His first release with them was "Two Hearts, Two Kisses." Obviously, the June 1955 release of "Ain't That a Shame" was historic and paved the way to a list of recording hits that extended from early rock 'n' roll to the beach songs of the mid-sixties.

On his family shows on TV, Pat introduced his wife Shirley and four daughters to North American audiences. Teaming up with daughter Debbie in the seventies proved to be a successful move. Debbie's recording of the theme from the movie *You Light Up My Life* propelled her to stardom almost instantly. Today Debbie can be seen on TV specials and she has appeared with a touring company performing Broadway shows.

Conway Twitty (left) was an Elvis copycat. Vancouver, 1962.

Brian "Frosty" Forst, Del Shannon, and I at C-FUN, Vancouver, 1962.

CHUM Toronto promotion party with Gordon Lightfoot, Pat Hervey, Peggy (Keenan) Hodgins, Mike Darrow, Bob McAdorey, Bob Laine and the late Al Boliska.

With my pal Bob Luman, Vancouver, 1962.

Everyone knew Johnny Ray as the "Prince of Wails." Vancouver, 1962.

1962

In addition to meeting Pat Boone, I began six exciting years at C-FUN Radio in Vancouver on April 1, 1962. C-FUN was just that — fun. A new decade, a new station and a delicious set of call letters — the best in Canada — made the challenge inviting.

The station caused a stir during the reign of rock 'n' roll; even The *New York Times* did a piece on it. Travel writer John M. Lee visited Vancouver and offered his view of the West Coast in an article printed in the *Times* in August 1966:

> English Bay is a Canadian Copacabana, a beach rimmed with swank apartment towers and crowned on a sunny Sunday with bikinis, muscle men, folk singers, frolicking children and elderly women sunning on brown benches. *All* the transistor radios seemed tuned to a rock and roll station called C-FUN, pronounced sea-fun.

In 1962, I was appearing on the CBC TV show "Cross Canada Hit Parade," which I thoroughly enjoyed. One program featured former Ottawa deejay Rich Little (yes, *the* Rich Little) and the late Toronto deejay Al Boliska. Boliska, who worked for CHUM Toronto at the time, was infamous in Canada for his collection of the world's worst jokes. Trust me, they were! If you really want to check, ask your record store for Al's album — it's still selling.

I didn't know Rich Little at the time; nor it appears, did any other broadcasters. Around that time, Rich had applied to CHUM Toronto for a job as an afternoon deejay. Program Director Allan Slaight told his assistant, Peggy (Keenan) Hodgins, to "let him off the hook gently. The guy really doesn't have it." And he hired Global TV commentator Bob McAdorey instead.

Rich, Al and I did the show together and afterwards, in a spirited mood, Al called for a cab to take us downtown. Recognizing Al's name, the cabbie turned to Rich and said, "I love your morning show, Boliska. You're the funniest guy in town." With that, Rich Little carried on as if he were Boliska. When the cabbie asked who the other two were, I said I was myself and Boliska said he was Rich Little. The cabbie commented, "Nice names." Finally, the real Boliska asked the

1962

cabbie if he had heard Al Boliska (Rich Little) do his impressions. Rich then launched into a whole series of impressions — Kirk Douglas, Burt Lancaster, James Mason, Jimmy Stewart and the rest of his repertoire of the time. The cabbie told Rich he should do more of these on his morning show and Rich agreed.

During another appearance on that TV show I met Gordon Lightfoot, a Toronto country-folk singer who had been performing at the Riverboat Club. Gordon was a true vagabond and his talents were largely regional in appeal until the late seventies, when he made *Billboard*'s Top 100 with his composition "If You Could Read My Mind." He is now considered the definitive Canadian folksinger/songwriter, Canada's answer to Bob Dylan. While Dylan was writing about the American dream, Lightfoot was writing odes to the mountains, forests and prairies. His music reflects this country.

Gordon Lightfoot's folk masterpiece, "The Canadian Railroad Trilogy," tells best of his love for Canada. Lightfoot will not accept the traditional Gold Leaf Award for Canadian record sales of 25,000 copies. He insists that sales must surpass 100,000 copies. When that happens, his record company makes up a special award and presents it to him. He's a star all right, but he always acts like the pleasant, retiring person that he is. We're proud of him.

Meanwhile, back on the West Coast, Bobby Curtola's appearance at the Kitsilano Showboat event with the C-FUN Good Guys drew over 10,000 to the edge of a Vancouver beach one hot summer's night back in the early sixties. A remarkable crowd in those days — especially when you consider Bobby was a Canadian!

Stars would go anywhere to help hype their records, especially if they were just starting out. They would jump in a car with the station promotion director, a tape recorder, and cameras and drive around the city. While they were being promoted on the air, they were also greeting the people, who, in those days, hadn't been saturated with television appearances and therefore still found a bit of magic in the personal promotion tour.

In general, 1962 was not a year that stands out. But the best was just around the corner.

Top Ten Hits

1. Surfin' U.S.A. — The Beach Boys
2. End of the World — Skeeter Davis
3. Rhythm of the Rain — The Cascades
4. He's So Fine — The Chiffons
5. Blue Velvet — Bobby Vinton
6. Hey, Paula — Paul and Paula
7. Fingertips, Part Two — Stevie Wonder
8. Can't Get Used to Losing You — Andy Williams
9. My Boyfriend's Back — The Angels
10. Sukiyaki — Kyu Sakamoto

Grammy Awards

Record of the Year — *"The Days of Wine and Roses"* (Henry Mancini)

Album of the Year — *The Barbra Streisand Album* (Barbra Streisand)

Song of the Year — *"The Days of Wine and Roses"* (Henry Mancini and Johnny Mercer)

Best Male Vocalist — *Jack Jones* ("Wives and Lovers")

Best Female Vocalist — *Barbra Streisand* ("The Barbra Streisand Album")

Best Vocal Group — *Peter, Paul and Mary* ("Blowin' in the Wind")

Top Movies

Tom Jones
8½
Cleopatra
Irma La Douce
America, America
How the West Was Won
Hud
It's a Mad, Mad, Mad, Mad World
Dr. No
Lilies of the Field
The L-Shaped Room

On Broadway

Who's Afraid of Virginia Woolf?
The Milk Train Doesn't Stop Here Any More
Oliver
Stop the World, I Want to Get Off

The Oscars

Best Picture	*Tom Jones*
Best Director	Tony Richardson *(Tom Jones)*
Best Actor	Sidney Poitier *(Lilies of the Field)*
Best Actress	Patricia Neal *(Hud)*
Best Supporting Actor	Melvyn Douglas *(Hud)*
Best Supporting Actress	Margaret Rutherford
Best Song	*"Call Me Irresponsible"* by Jimmy Van Heusen and Sammy Cahn from *Papa's Delicate Condition*

On Television

Password
  (with Allen Ludden)
House Party
  (with Art Linkletter)
Route 66
Sing Along with Mitch
Mr. Novak
The Virginians
Ozzie & Harriet

Best Sellers

The Group
  Mary McCarthy

Happiness Is a Warm Puppy
  Charles Schultz

I Owe Russia $1200
  Bob Hope

The Glass Blowers
  Daphne du Maurier

The Fire Next Time
  James Baldwin

1963

One word sums up the beginning of 1963 — Motown. Berry Gordy's Motown recording studio started out like any other business that is to be successful — carefully, cautiously, and creatively. Unlike most businessmen, however, Berry singlehandedly represented, promoted and produced records by recording artists who often dominated the monthly Top 20 in sales and popularity and who had endurance as well. When it got rolling, Motown seemed to have all the power of the city of Detroit behind it.

Just a handful of the groups that Gordy promoted were Martha and the Vandellas, who recorded "Heat Wave" in 1963, Marvin Gaye and Smokey Robinson and the Miracles, whose hit "You've Really Got a Hold on Me" held a spot in the Top 50. But it was Stevie Wonder and Diana Ross and the Supremes who gave Motown that energy that has stood the test of time for over 20 years.

In 1963, a 12-year-old boy named Steveland Hardaway, who had been blind since birth, was entertaining friends and colleagues with his harmonica playing. That year he was discovered by Berry Gordy, who changed Steveland's name to Stevie Wonder and recorded his album *The Twelve-Year-Old Genius*. That album included a version of a Ray Charles hit, "Fingertips, Part Two," which became a top song during the year, holding down the number seven spot.

Like the Beatles, Elvis and only a few other composer-entertainers in the world, Stevie has gone on and on; his "wonderment" has never stopped. He is an incredible talent whose roots are solidly in rock 'n' roll; yet he could pen such romantic tunes as "My Cherie Amour" and "You Are the Sunshine of My Life." He is another star who is best known for the songs he writes and records himself.

The top song of 1963 was by the Beach Boys. If you thought you'd heard "Surfin' U.S.A." someplace else, you were right. It was originally a Chuck Berry composition and hit called "Sweet Little Sixteen." The first pressing of the record "Surfin' U.S.A." attributed the song to Brian Wilson of the Beach Boys. A quick call from the company holding the rights to Chuck Berry's song encouraged a revision on the record label and the record is now rightfully credited to Chuck Berry.

1963

Whether or not this was a case of two people hearing the same kind of music has never been established. You'll often hear new lyrics to an old song. When the song has been copyrighted, however, credit must be given to the copyright holder. A lengthy court battle established that "My Sweet Lord," which George Harrison released as his own, was composed by R. Mack as "He's So Fine," which the Chiffons recorded. To this day, both renditions of the song are played. Royalties go to the original author — the guy who wrote "He's So Fine."

In the middle of the twisting, the surfing and the Bossa Nova — in addition to the steady old rock that was still being played — there was a whole raft of songs that fit into a category I call "candy sweet" music. It didn't last but was popular for a brief period. Just a few examples are "Roses Are Red," "Our Day Will Come," "Blue on Blue," and "Can't Get Used to Losing You."

Some groups both sang alone and backed up the stars in recording stints and during the many international promotional tours that took place in those days. The Angels, the Cookies, the Bobbettes, the Ronettes, the Crystals, the Janettes and the Chiffons were just a few of these groups. They came into their own again briefly when Barbra Streisand did a parody of these groups in "A Star Is Born" (the third and, in my opinion, the best, remake of the movie) and acted as one of a trio of singers called the Oreos.

Now it was truly fashionable to twist. Even a mild bit of rock 'n' rolling was acceptable. After all, members of the Elvis generation were grown up and living in suburbia, and they weren't about to admit they were over the hill because they were in their twenties and thirties. Even the socialites got into the act. I refer to the lovely Leslie Gore, a rich New Yorker who sang "It's My Party (and I'll Cry If I Want to)" and "Judy's Turn to Cry." She was good — not great, but good. From coast to coast, the continent was twisting, rocking and enjoying the "now" music.

Remember the Rooftop Singers? They had a hit on their hands with "Walk Right In," which kept folk music alive that year, as did "If I Had a Hammer," the old Pete Seeger hit. That song had been recorded quite successfully by Peter, Paul and Mary in 1962 and was recorded again in 1963 by Trini Lopez, whose album *Live at P.J.'s* (a

Pat Boone was a popular visitor to the Cave. This photo was taken in 1963.

Jimmie Rodgers promotes his latest LP at C-FUN in 1963.

Bobby Curtola talks to C-FUN listeners, 1963.

The Crickets after Buddy Holly in Vancouver, April 28, 1963. From left, Glenn D. Hardin (Elvis's pianist/organist until his death), Sonny Curtis (composer of the theme song for "The Mary Tyler Moore Show"), Jerry Naylor (now a KLAC deejay in L.A.), and Jerry Allison (Buddy Holly's original drummer.)

1963

nightclub in Los Angeles) told you where he recorded. The Chicano lilt of Lopez added a lot to the basic common-sense Seeger approach, and the song reached a wide-ranging audience. Even today, it remains a popular sing-along number.

Every year a sentimental song emerges as the song people danced to and fell in love to. You couldn't go anywhere in 1963 without hearing the poignant Henry Mancini tune "The Days of Wine and Roses." This song always evokes powerful emotional memories for anyone who saw the movie from which the song was taken. It quite rightly won the Academy Award for best song of the year.

Henry Mancini has probably won more Oscars and Grammys than almost any other artist. His first was for "Mr. Lucky" in 1960. "Moon River" was featured in *Breakfast at Tiffany's*, which is Truman Capote's most famous movie production after *In Cold Blood*. Henry's remarkable ability and range is apparent when you consider his string of hits: "Charade," "Pink Panther Theme," "Dear Heart" (which put Andy Williams on the Top 10 charts), "Love Story," and the "Theme from Charlie's Angels."

After Buddy Holly died, the Crickets were still performing. But, like many other groups, they went through a series of changes. When I met them in 1963, the new Crickets had been joined by my good friend Jerry Naylor, who took the lead singer's role, left vacant by Buddy's death. Today Jerry is a deejay at KLAC radio, Los Angeles.

Jerry Allison, the drummer, was the only one of the original Crickets to remain with the group. One of the other original members, Glen D. Harden, later became Elvis Presley's pianist on his Las Vegas shows and concert tour — a position he held until Elvis's death in 1977.

While the Crickets toured British Columbia in a C-FUN-sponsored promotion, the McGuire Sisters had an "SRO" play at the Cave Supper Club. Their 1954 hit "Sincerely" had been a cover version of the rhythm and blues hit by the Moonglows. One of the first cover groups in the business, the McGuire Sisters had a number of hits until 1963, when they disbanded. Later, Phyllis toured on her own. I met the McGuire Sisters in 1963 and was struck by their beauty, personality and talent.

1963

Les Vogt and I were partners at Jaguar, our booking enterprise in those days, and that year Les put the team of Johnny and Dorsey Burnette in a package with Donnie Brooks for a tour of the Vancouver area. These Tennessee boys almost tore a hotel room to bits during their visit. I was called in by an upset hotel manager in Vancouver's English Bay in the wee small hours of the morning. After some fast talking, I was able to convince him to let them stay for the rest of the night. But let me tell you, that room was a mess. Even in those days rock 'n' roll stars wrecked hotel rooms.

The Burnette brothers enjoyed fishing and were nearly drowned in English Bay, downtown Vancouver's fishing ground. Fortunately, they were saved by an alert coast guard. By a horrible coincidence, Johnny did drown on a Lake Meade fishing trip only a year later on August 1, 1964.

These guys were original rock 'n' rollers. With their friend Paul Burlison, they had formed the Johnny Burnette Trio back in 1956. Their first Coral label releases were not hits. In 1957, they headed for California, where they began writing material for Imperial recording artist Rick Nelson and for Roy Brown. Dorsey started off with "The Tall Oak Tree" in early 1960, while Johnny had his first big hit, "Dreamin'," on Liberty Records the same year.

In 1961, they recorded "The Green Grass of Texas," a smash hit, as the Texans. They used their own names after that, but Dorsey had just two hits, "The Tall Oak Tree" and "Hey, Little One." Johnny's hits included "Dreamin'," "You're Sixteen," "Little Boy Sad," "Big, Big World" and "God, Country and My Baby." As for Donnie Brooks, who was also on that triple bill, he had several hits, including "Mission Bell," "Doll House" and "Memphis."

These three were wild characters offstage. The minute they hit that stage, however, they were all business. They were three of the most memorable singers and entertainers during the pre-Beatle era. Despite their antics, they remain among my all-time favorites.

Chubby Checker also came to Vancouver in 1963. When he taught you how to twist, you didn't forget. He had all of the C-FUN Good Guys on stage with him at Isy's Supper Club and insisted that we try it with him. We did. The audience cracked up — Tom Peacock, Al Jordan, Frosty Forst and I were not noted for our dance floor

Roy Orbison was the number one star after Elvis in the early sixties. Shown without the famous shades in Vancouver, 1963.

Johnny Burnett, Dorsey Burnett, and Donnie Brooks at C-FUN, 1963.

The McGuire Sisters at the Cave. From left, Chris McGuire, me, Phyllis McGuire, Glen Hardin, Dottie McGuire, and Jerry Naylor.

1963

agility. Chubby was a fine showman. He had a talent for impressions, which he performed during his stay in Vancouver, both on stage and off.

The twist craze lasted for about three years, during which Chubby gained an international reputation. His 10-year run ended in the spring of 1969 with his recording of the Beatles' composition "Back in the U.S.S.R."

Besides the twist, Chubby is also responsible for the introduction of such dances as the hucklebuck, the pony and the fly. It has been reported that Dick Clark's wife suggested the name "Checker" after seeing Chubby on "American Bandstand." Chubby's real name is Ernest Evans.

When Mel Carter came to town in 1964, the female audience at the Cave — and at a live appearance at the old Orpheum Theatre — fell firmly in lust with him. Mel's hits from June 1963 through the fall of 1966 included "When a Boy Falls in Love," "Hold Me, Thrill Me, Kiss Me" (a remake of the hit recording of the fifties that brought success to Kitty Kallen, lead singer at one point with the Harry James Orchestra, "All of a Sudden My Heart Sings," "Love Is All We Need," "Band of Gold," "You, You, You" (another remake of the Ames Brothers' fifties hit) and "Take Good Care of Her." Despite his sexy personality, excellent promotional team and attractive ballad style, Mel's intense recording popularity didn't survive those desperate sixties.

Johnny Mathis can't be considered a rock 'n' roller in any way. But even in 1963 his soft ballad style provided a pleasant contrast to the pounding beat of the fifties that had carried over into the sixties. That style has made him one of the most enduring balladeers of the last three decades.

In the early sixties, there weren't many female voices on private radio. To do something different, I asked our promotion director, Peggy (Keenan) Hodgins, to interview Mathis for our C-FUN audience. Peggy had interviewed dozens of stars, including Harry Belafonte, Peter, Paul and Mary, Cliff Richard, Gordon Lightfoot, Tony Bennett and many more. Her Mathis interview remains as a permanent piece of my nostalgia collection.

Interestingly, Johnny made news again in the recording

1963

industry in 1982 with another sixties favorite, Dionne Warwick. Their duet, "Friends in Love," is a clear indication of their individual and joint talents.

Dionne was discovered by Burt Bacharach, who introduced her to Florence Greenbert, the president of Scepter Records. Greenbert gave her a contract. Dionne recorded Bacharach's song, with Hal David's lyrics, "Don't Make Me Over" in 1962, launching the relationship that saw a batch of hits for the three of them over the next 10 years.

From "Walk On By" in 1964 to "Make It Easy on Yourself" in 1970, the voice of Dionne Warwick has made Bacharach-David music known to all ages of music lovers. In between those hits came "Message to Michael" and "Trains and Boats and Planes" in 1966, "Alfie" in 1967, "Do You Know the Way to San Jose?" in 1968 and "This Girl's in Love with You" in 1969. Bacharach no longer writes with Hal David but with his wife, Carol Bayer Sager. Their theme song from *Arthur* shows that Bacharach can write music for every decade.

When Jack Jones dropped into C-FUN for interviews in 1963, you couldn't see through the control room window for the mass of females who had gathered to stare at this handsome singer. Jack's father was operatic singer Allan Jones, who had recorded the classic "Donkey Serenade." Jack's own first hit was "Lollipops and Roses," which won the Grammy Award in 1963 for the best pop single of the year. Some of his biggest hits were "Call Me Irresponsible," "Wives and Lovers," "The Race Is On," "Lady," and "The Impossible Dream." Jack's songs have a true romantic sound, but he can belt them out with a good beat when he wants.

When Jack visited Vancouver, his haughty attitude annoyed C-FUN secretary, Eva Corrin. To this day, she recalls reminding him that I was a busy man and couldn't drop everything just to greet him at the front door! Eva remembers that "he asked me if I knew who he was after I'd asked him to wait a minute before I could buzz Red to tell him Jack Jones was here (late) for the interview. So I replied, 'Yes, we know who you are. But do you know who Mr. Robinson is?' He was really quite annoyed."

I mention this exchange because in my view the real stars, the greats, are always on time if they can be (let's face it, anyone can

Interviewing Jack Jones at C-FUN in 1963.

Dick and Deedee visit the C-FUN studio to promote their latest LP, 1963.

The picture says it all. Red and Carol Robinson, Vancouver, May 1963.

The C-FUN Good Guys (from bottom left): Fred Latremouille, me, Tom Peacock, Brian "Frosty" Forst, Ed Kargle, and Al Jordan. Vancouver, 1963.

1963

be late on a promotional tour), and, more important, they're always pleasant to the secretaries and receptionists. In a radio station, I've seen the manager and even the owner spell off the hassled switchboard operator. So, in addition to being a matter of courtesy, it pays to be pleasant to whoever greets you out there.

Another Vancouver favorite was Frankie Laine, who dropped into town many times. Some people may ask, "What does Frankie Laine have to do with rock 'n' roll?" Frankie was a major figure in pop circles 10 years before rock 'n' roll struck. "That's My Desire" was his first national hit, in 1947, and he didn't stop recording hits until 1970. That's an amazing feat for anyone when you consider the fads that blew in and out during those decades. He will go down in the annals of pop music as one of the biggest and most successful commercial singers in the history of show business.

Frankie Laine had a voice so powerful he could be heard in a large auditorium with no microphone. In the midst of rock 'n' roll fever in 1957, he struck gold with two ballads, "Moonlight Gambler" and "Love Is a Golden Ring." In 1963 it was "Don't Make My Baby Blue," and in 1967, "I'll Take Care of Your Cares."

When Frankie came through Vancouver in 1963, I interviewed him on C-FUN before his engagement at the Cave Supper Club. He returned in 1966 and was interviewed by colleague Peggy (Keenan) Hodgins then at CKLG. We both enjoyed Frankie — he was an engaging personality. Peggy recalls that he was a gourmand and hosted a posh dinner party for the press at the Sir Walter Raleigh Restaurant to introduce his Manhandlers commercials. He told us he was on a diet at the time.

Novelty tunes again won favor with the record-buying public, and Allan Sherman swung to immediate stardom with his comical memo from camp, "Hello Muddah, Hello Faddah."

Rolf Harris would be the first to tell you that he got his big start in Vancouver at the Cave Supper Club. Impressario, Ben Kopelow is one of those show business traditions who loves talent and loves to promote good people. He met and admired Rolf and has been involved in the promotion of Rolf's career since 1963, when Rolf first appeared in town. Rolf had tremendous rapport with audiences and today he's a special citizen when he visits Vancouver. His unique

1963

ability with a wobble board and his attempts to give his material a local flavor help broaden his appeal. Add to that the fair number of Australians who live in or visit Vancouver and you realize why Rolf was an instant hit here.

"Tie Me Kangaroo Down, Sport" is Rolf's special signature and was a worldwide hit. Pat Boone tried to cover "Tie Me Kangaroo Down," but it was an unqualified bomb. There are some hits that can't be covered. The Rolf Harris kangaroo song is just one that needed to be sung by its original recording artist.

"Sun Arise" and "Vancouver Town" are two other songs synonymous with Rolf Harris around the world. Rolf is also active on the many telethons broadcast from the Vancouver area.

Bobby Goldsboro was relatively unknown when he first started touring with Roy Orbison's troupe. He had recorded "Molly" on Laurie Records, but it only reached number 70 on the *Cashbox* Top 100 in 1963. "See the Funny Little Clown" turned things around for Bobby in January 1964. It was an appropriate song for him because he was a natural clown. When he was in Vancouver in 1963 he drove all of us crazy by making the sound of a cricket with his voice. Since then, the cricket sound has been his calling card — you may have seen him on TV clowning around and making the sound on one of his many guest appearances.

I had originally met Bobby Bare at Ford Ord during my army stint there. Bobby was one of the country artists responsible for breaking down the barriers between country music and pop music with songs such as "Detroit City," "Shame on Me," and "500 Miles from Home." He also recorded the best seller "Four Strong Winds," written by Canadian guitarist Ian Tyson, who had been a member of the Stripes, a rock band I had formed and managed in the fifties. Ian Tyson is still visible in Canada as a TV and recording artist and Bobby remains in Nashville as a successful country performer.

Out of Portland, Oregon, came the Kingsmen, who recorded "Louie, Louie." If you know the song, you'll recall the nasal way of delivery that made it sound like "Lou-aye, Lou-aye."

I have always enjoyed and admired Roy Orbison and I remember remarking, in 1963, that he was one of the few guys on the

1963

charts that year who would still be around in 20 years. Orbison was one of the original Sun recording stars and was encouraged by none other than Pat Boone. His first hit, "Ooby Dooby," was followed by "Uptown," "Only the Lonely," "Blue Angel," "I'm Hurtin'," and the classic, "Running Scared," plus "Crying" and "Candy Man." These and others established Roy as one of the biggest chartbusters of the early sixties. By 1977, he had charted no fewer than 29 hits.

Roy brought Bob Luman, the country and western singer, Bobby Goldsboro and a new group later titled the Newbeats with him to Vancouver in 1963. The only action the Newbeats saw on national charts was with their novelty song, "Bread and Butter."

I met Paul Anka again in 1963 when he was in town with a huge-sounding band playing the Cave. Paul was riding high on the charts with the RCA hits "Love Me Warm and Tender," "A Steel Guitar, a Glass of Wine," "Every Night" and "Eso Beso." I can't stress enough the impact of Paul Anka on the entertainment field. He had written "It Doesn't Matter Anymore" for Buddy Holly in the fifties and it was this record that was played on February 3, 1959, the day Holly died in the plane crash near Fargo, North Dakota. This event was immortalized in the song "American Pie," which catapulted Don McLean from reasonable obscurity to instant fame when the song was released in 1972.

Paul Anka later wrote Frank Sinatra's theme song, "My Way," and a group of hits, including "She's a Lady" for Tom Jones. He infuriated feminists with the 1974 hit "(You're) Having My Baby," but that didn't stop the song or the album from selling. And every evening millions of North Americans, and not a few people overseas, are serenaded by the theme music Paul penned for *The Tonight Show* with Johnny Carson. As an entertainer, composer and business manager, Paul Anka is a giant in the entertainment world today.

As for the British influence, Cliff Richard was traipsing across Canada in 1963 promoting his record and his English-made movie at the same time. Handsome and popular, he was the closest England ever got to having a figure as strong as Elvis Presley. Twenty years later, Cliff Richard continues to be a popular singer. He made his comeback in 1976 with the song "Devil Woman."

1963

Meanwhile, in Germany, a motley group of musicians was appearing under the name of the Quarrymen. It wouldn't be long before they decided to pattern themselves after their heroes, Buddy Holly and the Crickets, and become the Beatles.

Overriding any other event in 1963 was the shattering news bulletin that stunned TV and radio audiences everywhere. John Kennedy, President of the United States, was assassinated while riding in a convertible with his wife, Jackie, at his side in Dallas, Texas.

Everyone who admired this youthful leader was numb. Ask anyone what he was doing that day and he'll be able to tell you — precisely. I was sleeping late when my wife, Carol, woke me and pulled me into the TV room to view the shocking events as they unfolded on the screen. I watched for a few minutes and then rushed into C-FUN, where I was program director, and grabbed the traffic manager, Barb Tisman (later Mrs. Bob Luman of Nashville fame). Together we changed the radio logs to full symphonic music and canceled all commercials for the day. People were in tears everywhere. Then I walked into the library and seized the best-selling Vaughan Meader *First Family* LP and "Hit the Road, Jack," which I also associated with Jack Kennedy and smashed them both. A generation of dreams was breaking along with the vinyl records. It was one of the most emotional moments of my life. What I couldn't predict at the time was the chain of events that was instantly set in motion and that would subsequently reflect the troubled sixties.

Despite that terrible tragedy, we managed to go on without the Kennedy spark. The songs ending the year included "Dominique" by the Singing Nun, "Forget Him" by Bobby Rydell, "Be True to Your School" by the Beach Boys and, fittingly, the one we'll recall as the most significant of the year, "The Times They Are A-Changin'" by Bob Dylan.

Top Ten Hits

1. *I Want to Hold Your Hand* — The Beatles
2. *She Loves You* — The Beatles
3. *Hello, Dolly* — Louis Armstrong
4. *Oh, Pretty Woman* — Roy Orbison
5. *I Get Around* — The Beach Boys
6. *Everybody Loves Somebody* — Dean Martin
7. *My Guy* — Mary Wells
8. *We'll Sing in the Sunshine* — Gale Garnett
9. *Last Kiss* — J. Frank Wilson and the Cavaliers
10. *Where Did Our Love Go?* — The Supremes

Grammy Awards

Record of the Year	"The Girl from Ipanema" (Stan Getz and Astrid Gilberto)
Album of the Year	*Getz/Gilberto* (Stan Getz and Astrid Gilberto)
Song of the Year	"Hello, Dolly" (Jerry Herman)
Best Male Vocalist	*Louis Armstrong* ("Hello, Dolly")
Best Female Vocalist	*Barbra Streisand* ("People")
Best Vocal Group	*The Beatles* ("A Hard Day's Night")

On Broadway

Hamlet
Any Wednesday
Hello, Dolly
Funny Girl
Fiddler on the Roof

On Television

I've Got a Secret
Naked City
Peyton Place
Kraft Suspense Theatre

Top Movies

My Fair Lady
Mary Poppins
The Unsinkable Molly Brown
Hush, Hush, Sweet Charlotte
A Hard Day's Night
Dr. Strangelove
Zorba the Greek
Seven Days in May
Father Goose
Goldfinger

The Oscars

Best Picture	*My Fair Lady*
Best Director	George Cukor (*My Fair Lady*)
Best Actor	Rex Harrison (*My Fair Lady*)
Best Actress	Julie Andrews (*Mary Poppins*)
Best Supporting Actor	Peter Ustinov (*Topkapi*)
Best Supporting Actress	Lila Kedrova (*Zorba the Greek*)
Best Song	"Chim Chim Cher-ee" by Richard M. Sherman and Robert B. Sherman from *Mary Poppins*

Best Sellers

The Moveable Feast
Ernest Hemingway

The Naked Society
Vance Packard

The Keeper of the House
Shirley A. Grau

Herzog
Saul A. Bellow

Little Big Man
Thomas Berger

1964

"Who are these guys, the Beatles?" I asked Jerry Naylor of the Crickets early in 1963. Jerry assured me that the Del Shannon hit "From Me to You" was one of the Beatles' hits in Great Britain. Jerry also told me that the group had selected their name as a tribute to the late Buddy Holly and his group, the Crickets.

I was skeptical. I played Jerry's copy of "From Me to You" in the C-FUN library. I wasn't impressed. But because Jerry was so enthusiastic, I decided to test the sound on the air and see if there was any response. Nothing happened. I didn't receive one phone call!

So that was my introduction to the Beatles in 1963. That all changed, however, in 1964, when the Beatles arrived with a bang heard around the world.

This talented band burst onto the scene and dominated the 1964 charts with "A Hard Day's Night," "Love Me Do," "Please, Please Me," "Twist and Shout," "Can't Buy Me Love," and "Do You Want to Know a Secret?" That's just the kind of reaction that Elvis had created back in 1957. Beatlemania had struck!

Interestingly, EMI, the recording company that first released the Beatles' records, had problems releasing the records in North America. (Some "astute" Capitol Record executives in Hollywood remarked that the Beatles were not really made for the American market.) Nevertheless, their first four singles shot to the top and became instant collectors' items. This really shook up the promotion people at EMI — and Brian Epstein, the man who had taken the Beatles on as a project and made them brush their hair, wear tidy clothes and clean up their act on stage.

A new era in entertainment had begun.

Contrary to popular belief, Ed Sullivan did not introduce North American television viewers to the Beatles. That honor belongs to Jack Parr, then host of the "Tonight Show," who had some film footage he had brought back from a British holiday. After Parr aired this footage, the Beatles appeared live on the "Ed Sullivan Show," creating total chaos. From that point on, because of the continuous screams and shouts and applause, I don't think anyone ever really heard an entire Beatles concert anywhere in the world. Anyone who attended those concerts will tell you, however, that there was an undeniable thrill in just being there — you could always listen to the records at home.

1964

On August 22, 1964, the Beatles headlined a concert in Vancouver. Those who were there will never forget it. As program director of C-FUN radio, I had selected popular young Vancouver deejay Fred Latremouille to represent C-FUN on stage and emcee the show. Fate struck when Freddie was unexpectedly hospitalized and I replaced him both at the Beatles press conference and at the concert.

I had some fun that day. This is how it was described in the September 19, 1964, issue of *Maclean's*:

The Ordeal of Ringo's Ringer

> By dawn of B-Day, the usual complement of teenage girls were asleep on waiting room benches at Vancouver International Airport, where the chartered Beatle airliner was scheduled to arrive later that day. About three thousand youngsters, most of them between ten and fourteen years, began an all-day vigil around the hotel. Many used lipstick to scrawl their names and Beatle slogans on the plywood barricades: some pre-pubescent girls threw themselves against the barrier and kissed it. Red Robinson, arbiter of the CFUNtastic fifty top tunes and Doyen of Vancouver Disk Jockeys, poured gasoline on troubled waters by hiring a boy who looked like Ringo Starr, outfitting him in a Beatle wig, and then broadcasting rumours that the drumming Beatle had been seen around town. When Ringo's ringer drove up to The Georgia Hotel, the youngsters mobbed his car. In the resultant confusions a girl was knocked down, one wheel of the car rolled over a policeman's foot and some teenage boys managed to swipe two revolvers from a policeman's holster. (Later that day, Robinson partially redeemed himself: At the insistence of police, he interrupted The Beatles' performance to broadcast an appeal for order from the stage microphone.)

Cool it or we'll cancel, I cautioned the crowd in Vancouver during the Beatles' 1964 tour.

John Lennon shouted, "F--- off, Red," in Vancouver at PNE sold-out crowd, August 22, 1964. (He later apologized.)

1964

People in Vancouver still remember the Ringo Starr stunt. Admittedly, it wasn't the brightest promotional move of my career. But we were carried away with Beatlemania, and in those days C-FUN was known for its bizarre and sensational promotional stunts. Yes, I should have used more discretion.

Good friend and late *Vancouver Sun* columnist Jack Wasserman reported, "The Beatles were on stage for a total of 29 minutes and 23 seconds. It took 35 minutes for the welcoming screams to die down enough for them to start. At one point Red Robinson, the local radio personality who M.C.'d, had to go on stage and tell the crowd to stop pressing forward."

The Beatles' manager, Brian Epstein, took a look at the wobbling stage front and the crowd pushing forward and shouted, "Red, get on stage and stop the show and tell those kids we won't go on if they don't calm down!"

I started to argue. I didn't want to get in front of that hysterical audience at all. Epstein shoved me onto the stage. As he did, Paul McCartney waved me off. Later, he told me that he thought that I thought the show was over. And when I arrived at the stage left mike, near John Lennon, John snarled, "Get the f--- off our stage! Nobody interrupts a Beatles performance!"

I tried to explain that Brian had asked me to interrupt the show, but John didn't want to listen. Paul yelled over, "That's all right, John. Brian says okay."

John replied, "Oh, why?" Because of the blinding kleig lights, he couldn't see the turmoil out front. After I explained the situation, he said, "Fine, but it's unusual. No one has ever done this before. There has never been a need." At that point, the show was stopped, the situation calmed down and the performance continued.

Meeting the Beatles in their trailer-dressing room before the show, I had the impression that Ringo was a lovable little guy with a good sense of humor. He didn't seem to take the whole Beatlemania thing seriously. Paul was quiet and thoughtful, as was George.

My opinion of John Lennon? He struck me as arrogant and pompous. He appeared to consider himself far above his peers and seemed to enjoy the inevitable media putdowns more than the other three. In my opinion, he saw himself as a clever intellectual. Never-

1964

theless, there is no doubting his phenomenal talent. His murder in December, 1980, was tragic.

The Beatles were the most extraordinary group to emerge during this century. Each one of them was totally individual, and their unusual combination of individuality made them unique. Their talents were varied and grew throughout the years. It is completely understandable to me why they eventually went off in their own directions. A four-way partnership of that magnitude could not survive.

The sound of rock in the early Beatle days was quite simple and straightforward. Known as the "Mersey sound" — in reference to the Mersey River, which flows through Liverpool — British rock 'n' roll in the initial stages was distinguished by its screaming fans, mop tops, and British accents. This was a hysterical period that would soon develop into something more involved and intricate.

Another of the original British groups to flash to international prominence was the Dave Clark Five, whom I also interviewed in 1964. Their big hit that year was "Glad All Over," which came out in February and rose to number six on *Billboard*'s Top 100. The Dave Clark Five didn't have the staying power of the Beatles, and that was obvious even then. They were not innovative, their music had a certain "sameness" about it and they could not create with the genius of the Beatles or the raw sensuality of the Rolling Stones. The Dave Clark Five followed so closely, however, that comparison to the Beatles' North American success was inevitable.

They played Vancouver on November 26, 1964, and herein lies another story showing the competitive nature of broadcasting. Sneaking into the rock field in Vancouver was an old competitor with a new rock sound, CKLG, which was trying to grab my C-FUN listeners. To counter this, I arranged for the Dave Clark Five to hold an exclusive press conference at C-FUN's studio.

Preparations were made to ensure a minimum of interruption from fans who might invade the station. So the first knowledge anyone had of the Dave Clark Five's presence in the studios was when they hit the air with the live press conference. Within minutes, CKLG was on the phone complaining bitterly to the promoters. We had an exclusive!

1964

There is nothing more fun than competition and certainly in 1964 the radio stations in Vancouver were in keen competition. CKLG was hounding C-FUN, and former C-FUN promotion director Peggy (Keenan) Hodgins had switched stations to help CKLG grow. Peggy was battling against her ex-C-FUN colleagues to boost the ratings and counter the C-FUN domination of the B.C. rock mart.

When C-FUN again captured another rock press conference and the on-stage emcee rights for the Rolling Stones concert, CKLG struck back in an imaginative way.

Peggy and CKLG deejays Roy Hennessy and Russ Simpson found out that we had hired two limousines to rush the Stones to downtown Vancouver for the well-publicized press conference. So Peggy hired three additional limos to confuse things at the arrival of the Rolling Stones' private jet at Vancouver International Airport. In those days, you could easily get on the tarmac and through the airport — security was not tight at all.

In the confusion, with five limos lined up, the chauffeurs were able to steer Mick Jagger and his bodyguard into one limo with Peggy and Russ, and some other members of the Rolling Stones into the limo with Roy Hennessy. Meanwhile, our C-FUN guys waited patiently upstairs and watched the proceedings from the airport arrival lounge, not realizing that CKLG was pulling a fast one on the ramp downstairs.

The procession looked like a funeral parade with the five black limousines and the CKLG and C-FUN news and promotion cruisers. I wouldn't have questioned anything at all except that, as usual, I was monitoring CKLG to find out what it was playing that hour. I heard one of the LG announcers saying, "And now, live from the airport, Roy Hennessy, Russ Simpson and Peggy Keenan with the first exclusive Vancouver interview with the Rolling Stones."

There was a commotion on the air and then I heard — as did all of CKLG's listeners — very clearly, a British voice demanding, "What the f--- do you think you're doing? I said no bloody mikes!"

There was the sound of a door opening and then the sound of that year's Rolling Stone hit, "Time Is on My Side." What none of us knew at that point was that the bodyguard had spotted Russ

John Lennon sings during the Beatles' 1964 concert at Empire Stadium in Vancouver.

1964

Simpson's microphone and Peggy's camera, which she had hidden in her purse. The triumphant trio was unceremoniously pushed out of the limousines into the inevitable Vancouver rain and had to walk back to their CKLG cruisers. But they had scooped C-FUN and I wasn't the least bit amused.

I personally found the Rolling Stones visit uneventful except for the capricious CKLG stunt. Mick Jagger was offensive and totally uncooperative with the C-FUN deejays. Remember, the Rolling Stones were a new band and needed the backup of North American radio stations — especially in a major market such as Vancouver. C-FUN's involvement was enormous. Jagger may have improved with time, but he left many disenchanted people in Vancouver.

The harsh rock sound and stylized stage appearance of the Rolling Stones made the Beatles seem like "pretty" or nice guys. Who could object to the happy sound of the Beatles singing "She Loves Me" after the pulsating, controversial lyrics of "Satisfaction"?

After the Beatles split up, the Rolling Stones became the world's number one rock band. Today they are still a phenomenon to see and hear. In those days many of us forgot that Mick Jagger had been a student at the London School of Economics. As a result, he is well versed in the ways of capitalism and high finance. In fact, at the beginning he went to school during the day and played in a band evenings — only when he was assured of a steady income did he become a full-time professional musician.

Certainly the Beatles and the Rolling Stones dominated the pop music scene in 1964. But there were others who had big hits and who are important in this romp down the musical memory lane.

From Motown Studios in Detroit came "Baby Love" with the Supremes, starring Diana Ross as lead singer. The Letterman sang "Goin' Out of My Head," and Ramsey Lewis had a jazz hit with "Hi-Heel Sneakers," which was also recorded by Jerry Lee Lewis.

One of the great things about entertainment — and, in particular, radio — is that it doesn't matter how much music or what type is on the Hit Parade. There's always room for another idea. Jazz buffs had long adored the genius of Stan Getz, but when he discovered Astrid Gilberto from Brazil and teamed up with the

The Beatles on stage at Vancouver's Empire Stadium, 1964.

The Beatles in Vancouver, 1964.

168   Vancouver loved the Dave Clark Five — 1964.

Chad and Jeremy, popular English duo, promoting "Yesterday's Gone." From left: Jeremy Clyde, "Jolly" John Tanner, and Chad Stewart. C-FUN, 1964.

1964

untrained folk singer for "The Girl from Ipanema" everyone jumped on the South American jazz train. The Getz/Gilberto sound was a superlative combination.

Another 1964 hit belonged to Barbra Streisand, whose rendition of "People" from the Broadway musical *Funny Girl* and later the Hollywood film of the same name remains unparalleled. Some songs done by a "cover" have been as good as the original recording. Both the Doors and José Feliciano did excellent work on "Light My Fire," for example. No one, however, has ever come close to matching Streisand's recording of "People." It was a pleasant diversion from the Beatles, the Rolling Stones, Gerry and the Pacemakers and the Four Tops.

Singing their own compositions were Bobby Vinton, who had written "Mister Lonely" with Gene Allan, Bob Dylan with "It Ain't Me, Babe", Roy Orbison, who had written "Oh, Pretty Woman" with Bill Dees and Gale Garnett, who is probably remembered exclusively for "We'll Sing in the Sunshine."

Joan Baez sang — and later recorded — "The House of The Rising Sun," a traditional American folk song with words and music by Alan Price. In 1964, non-folk followers enjoyed this song with a definite rock flavor by Eric Burdon and the Animals.

Could we imagine Lorne Greene singing a tribute to "Ringo"? He did, and it reached the charts in late December 1964. The Zombies drew attention to their talent with "She's Not There," and my old pals the Drifters managed to hit the charts with "Under the Boardwalk" — a catchy tune that would be part of the rock 'n' roll renaissance of the eighties.

It has been said that the only reason many of these records reached the top spots at all in the late sixties was because the Beatles couldn't keep up with the demand for their music. Their Christmas present to their fans was *Beatles '65*. It was a sign of things to come from the four who were unquestionably the top entertainment story of 1964.

Top Ten Hits

1. Woolly Bully — Sam the Sham and the Pharoahs
2. I Can't Help Myself — The Four Tops
3. Satisfaction — The Rolling Stones
4. You Were on My Mind — The We Five
5. You've Lost That Loving Feeling — The Righteous Brothers
6. Downtown — Petula Clark
7. Help — The Beatles
8. Can't You Hear My Heart Beat — Herman's Hermits
9. Crying in the Chapel — Elvis Presley
10. My Girl — The Temptations

Grammy Awards

Record of the Year — *"A Taste of Honey"* (Herb Alpert)
Album of the Year — *September of My Years* (Frank Sinatra)
Song of the Year — *"The Shadow of your Smile* (Paul Francis Webster and Johnny Mandel)
Best Male Vocalist — *Frank Sinatra* ("September of My Years")
Best Female Vocalist — *Barbra Streisand* (My Name is Barbra)
Best Vocal Group — *Anita Kerr Singers* (We Dig Mancini)

Top Movies

The Sound of Music
A Thousand Clowns
A Patch of Blue
The Spy Who Came In from the Cold
Those Magnificent Men in Their Flying Machines
The Greatest Story Ever Told
Help
Doctor Zhivago
Cat Ballou
The Sandpiper
Ship of Fools
King Rat
The Great Race
Darling

On Television

Get Smart
  (with Don Adams)
Gidget
Green Acres
Big Valley
Hogan's Heroes
Ed Sullivan
FBI

The Oscars

Best Picture	*The Sound of Music*
Best Director	Robert Wise (*The Sound of Music*)
Best Actor	Lee Marvin (*Cat Ballou*)
Best Actress	Julie Christie (*Darling*)
Best Supporting Actor	Martin Balsam (*A Thousand Clowns*)
Best Supporting Actress	Shelley Winters (*A Patch of Blue*)
Best Song	"The Shadow of Your Smile" by Johnny Mandel and Paul Francis Webster from *The Sandpiper*

On Broadway

The Odd Couple
On a Clear Day, You Can See Forever
The Roar of the Greasepaint, the Smell of the Crowd
Man of La Mancha
Half a Sixpence

Best Sellers

The Man
  Irving Wallace

Hotel
  Arthur Hailey

Yes, I Can
  Sammy Davis

Games People Play
  Eric Berne

Up the Down Staircase
  Bel Kaufman

The Green Berets
  Robin Moore

1965

Don't be fooled by the fact that Sam the Sham and the Pharoahs captured first place in the 1965 chart sweepstakes with "Woolly Bully." The Beatles were a strong influence in the music world and everyone was trying hard to keep up with the most innovative group since Buddy Holly and the Crickets. In fact, many compared the Beatles' work to that of Buddy Holly.

It was Bob Dylan, however, who grabbed the headlines at the Newport Folk Festival in 1965 by appearing with a rock band complete with electric guitar. This was considered sacrilege by the folk purists — none of their heroes had ever played with anything more than an acoustic guitar. They accused Dylan of selling out. It was at the festival that Dylan introduced the Band, a group of musicians who joined him after leaving as backup for Rompin' Ronnie Hawkins and the Hawks, who entertained out of Toronto. Again, it was a complete departure for a folk singer to have such a rompin' rockin' band as backup. Despite the shock of his electric guitar, Dylan drew a mammoth following and became even more popular with the release of his biggest hit, "Like a Rolling Stone."

If you put a flag beside the name of each recording artist or group in the Top 100 that year, the Union Jack would dominate. The Beatles paved the way to success for many a group that otherwise wouldn't have received much attention.

"Mrs. Brown, You've Got a Lovely Daughter" put Herman's Hermits on the charts for a while. They also had a novelty tune, "I'm Henry VIII, I Am," which deejays loved to play. The Seekers, Gerry and the Pacemakers, Shirley Bassey and the Dave Clark Five were just a few of the British imports on pop charts throughout the world. As if that weren't enough, country singer Roger Miller wrote and recorded "England Swings," the ultimate tribute to that country's entertainers.

Out of England also came a sexy singer by the name of Tom Jones, who recorded the Burt Bacharach and Hal David tune "What's New Pussycat?" for the movie of the same name (which starred Peter Sellers), establishing himself as a promising newcomer. Tom is one of my favorite entertainers because he's a true professional — like Paul Anka, Frank Sinatra, Elvis Presley and the handful of other people who command, or did command, top dollars because they are the

1965

ultimate performers. Unfortunately, Tom Jones has made too many television specials and guest shots. Although he is a best seller in Las Vegas, his TV appearances are rarely worth watching. Some people are dynamite on TV as well as in person and on stage, but Tom does not come across well on TV — as his ratings continually prove.

Petula Clark was another British import. You couldn't drive anywhere that year without hearing her toe-tapping Tony Hatch hit "Downtown." It was a lyrical, easy-listening tune that jumped the categories and was played on both AM and FM stations. She followed this up with another Tony Hatch composition, "I Know a Place," followed by "My Love," "I Couldn't Live without Your Love," "This Is My Song" and "Don't Sleep in the Subway," among others. She never really achieved superstar status because the competition from Barbra Streisand, Diana Ross and the Supremes and even Cher was too strong. She appeared in dozens of TV shows, however, and today she is still a fine performer and lyrical singer.

My old pals from Oregon, the Kingsmen, spoofed frozen food a bit with their recording "The Jolly Green Giant." As further proof that the world always needs a good novelty tune, Shirley Ellis is best recalled for a silly ditty known as "The Name Game," which I file under the "each-to-his-own-taste" category. Shirley never did become a major name in the recording industry after that release.

Salvatore Bono and Cherilyn LaPierre were background singers for Phil Spector and his recording house. They were on many records as nameless voices. Salvatore wrote "Needles and Pins" for Jackie DeShannon and this song was also recorded by the Searchers in England. In 1964, Cherilyn did a solo called "I Love You, Ringo" under the name of Bonnie Jo Mason. At one point, the two singers were known as Caesar and Cleo.

In 1965, they toured for ATCO (the Bobby Darin and Ray Charles recording house) and introduced "I Got You, Babe." The song was written by Sonny Bono, which is what Salvatore changed his name to. As Sonny and Cher, the duo toured as a warm-up act for various performers and began to attract national attention. They played Vancouver as a warm-up act in the midsixties, and many of the media people backstage interviewing them recall the innovative handmade clothes they both wore. Cher's fur jacket had been

Chubby Checker and CKLG jock Dave Palmer.

The Platters were anything but pretenders — they were great! Shown here with former C-FUN deejay (now a deejay in Toronto) Ron Grimster in Vancouver, 1965.

Marvin Gaye judges CKLG Crazy Hat Contest at the old Orpheum.

Paul Anka stops by the C-FUN reception desk in Vancouver, October 1965.

Sonny and Cher being interviewed backstage by CKLG deejay Roy Hennessy. Cher's in the middle.

Two of the five Beach Boys pose with C-FUN deejay "Jolly" John Tanner (middle). Left: Al Jardine. Right: Mike Love. Vancouver, 1965.

1965

handstitched, none too professionally, and both were more outlandish than the fashion plate image they project today.

Sonny and Cher were a pleasant duo and worked hard, but, except for Cher's extraordinary beauty, you wouldn't really classify them as unique. They also appeared in a sixties movie, *Wild on the Beach*, along with drummer Sandy Nelson. Of course it wasn't too long before they were the hot numbers in touring, in Las Vegas and on television. Cher went on to achieve superstar status and has emerged as an amazingly diverse talent since those days of Caesar and Cleo. To go from backup singer to Broadway actress is no small step. As for Sonny, he has found his niche as a successful restauranteur in Los Angeles.

Phil Spector, who had signed Sonny and Cher and many others, was a genius with sound. He had a remarkable ability to arrange a song in the most effective way. He also produced and directed many songs, including the Righteous Brothers' bit hit, "You've Lost That Lovin' Feeling," written by Cynthia Weill and Barrie Mann. To this day, the arrangements remain timely. (The Buddy Holly hit "It Really Doesn't Matter Any More" is another example of a well-produced and ideally arranged number that could have been recorded decades after it actually was, in the late fifties.)

Tom and Jerry had appeared on the Dick Clark radio show in 1957 and had also recorded the Mercury label hit "Hey! School Girl." At that time, they were receiving moderate attention on radio playlists. In 1965, they signed a Columbia recording contract and went on to become international entertainers using their real names — Paul Simon and Art Garfunkel. During the last week of December, 1965, they reached the charts with Paul's composition "Sounds of Silence." This song came from an album called *Wednesday Morning, 3 a.m.*, which did not do well, and Simon and Garfunkel went their separate ways for a short time after its release. During that period, a deejay discovered the "Sounds of Silence" cut on the album and played it. It caught the attention of Columbia Records, who decided to release it again as a single record. It was the first release to go "gold" for Simon and Garfunkel.

In 1967, the song was used as background music for *The Graduate* along with other songs Simon and Garfunkel wrote for the

1965

movie — all of which won them a Grammy for best original score for a motion picture. Simon and Garfunkel are probably best known for their recordings of "Mrs. Robinson" (from *The Graduate*), "59th Street Bridge Song" and "Bridge over Troubled Waters." After disbanding and again going their separate ways, they reunited for a 1982 concert in Central Park in New York City, which attracted hundreds of thousands of their fans. Since then, they have continued to record both separately and together.

One of the first folk-rock records to make an impact on the charts was the Bob Dylan composition "Mr. Tambourine Man," performed and made popular in 1965 by the Byrds, whose 1966 recording of Pete Seeger's "Turn, Turn, Turn" also made the charts. Though they disbanded in the early seventies, the members who originally formed the Byrds are still active today. One of the Byrds, David Crosby, went on to become a founding member of Crosby, Stills and Nash.

Despite all this fine music, the Beatles dominated the sounds everywhere. We couldn't escape their music — especially when all the easy-listening stations began playing instrumental versions of their releases. One of their biggest and earliest fans was the late and legendary Arthur Fiedler, whose Boston Pops recording of the Beatles' hits still sells today.

The Beatles embarked on a second North American tour launched at Shea Stadium in New York City, with the late Murray the K, a New York deejay who called himself the "fifth Beatle," as emcee. This tour took place before Woodstock and has been called the birth of the rock festival. The Beatles' take was the biggest gross in the history of show business up until that time.

In Vancouver, CKLG launched the first of two Beatle Bus contests. One entire boardroom at the station was crammed with entries from anxious Beatle fans who wanted to win that trip to Portland with the CKLG deejays to see the sold-out performance. What amazed the station's contest officials was the ingenuity of the entries — one sketch of Paul McCartney stood over eight feet tall!

If you recall the Lovin' Spoonful, whose hit that year was "Do You Believe in Magic?", then maybe you'll be interested in knowing that John Sebastian of that group recorded the theme song to

1965

"Welcome Back, Kotter" for the Gabriel Kaplan TV series that launched John Travolta.

Barbers were going crazy in 1965 as American, Canadian and British youth tried to copy the Beatles' "private school" haircut. On many, it was flattering — especially the guys. The result was the demise of the standard barber as young men sought out hair stylists.

Radio had been changing throughout the years and in 1965 "boss radio" originated at station KHJ in Los Angeles, revolutionizing rock radio. Boss radio was a clean, tight, scripted programming policy with absolutely no dead air. It required a rapid-fire delivery and few deejays were able to maintain their identity unless they worked at it. Two who gained fame in the United States were Robert W. Morgan and Sam Riddel, who used fractions of minutes to impart something witty, wise, or informative. The name "boss radio" came from the L.A. expression "Hey, man, you're boss," which is what someone said if he liked you. The expression took on yet another meaning when the KHJ deejays began announcing the time, temperature and other information as it related to "Boss" Angeles.

This type of radio was fine for the mega markets such as Los Angeles, San Francisco and New York, but when Canadian programmers adapted it in Toronto and Vancouver, it narrowed the choices for those who wanted popular music but didn't necessarily want the teenage hip and hard delivery of boss radio. In Canada, a small number of radio stations are allowed in each market — at that time, there were about seven in the Vancouver area. With two stations trying to be boss, the listeners didn't have much choice.

The Vancouver appearance of the Beach Boys in January, 1965, was one of many appearances in the city for the surfin' sons of California. And it brought two other fine recording artists to our attention.

Charlie Rich was among the headliners of the show. To most of the record-buying public, Charlie was an unknown. But he had been a favorite of mine since March, 1960, when his recording of "Lonely Weekends" was released on the Sun label. Charlie was a fine singer, but his talents were not really appreciated until the seventies when he began adding award after award to his collection, following two giant hits, "Behind Closed Doors" and "The Most Beautiful Girl."

1965

Here is a man whose "overnight" success had taken 15 years. If you're a bonafide record collector, you'll appreciate some of Charlie's earlier material on the Phillips, Mercury and RCA labels. Whether he is belting blues, rock 'n' roll, or country, the soul of Charlie Rich comes shining through, as it did at that concert in 1965.

With Charlie Rich at the Beach Boys' 1965 concert was another relatively unknown recording artist — Glen Campbell. (He was well known in recording studios, but not to the public.) Filling in for ailing lead singer Brian Wilson of the Beach Boys, Glen played the guitar and sang with the group. It wasn't until 1965, however, that he made it to the charts with a whopper, "Universal Soldier," written by Canadian singer-composer Buffy St. Marie.

Glen had charted "Turn Around, Look at Me" in 1961, and "Too Late to Worry, Too Blue to Cry" in 1962. When Glen first recorded "Gentle on My Mind" in 1967 it didn't do that well, though it did make some of the regional charts. In 1968, however, it hit the *Billboard* charts and took off. After this, Glen produced a string of hits and teamed up with songwriter Jimmy Webb to make musical history with songs such as "By the Time I Get to Phoenix," "Wichita Lineman" and "Galveston." Glen is a true survivor in the shark-infested entertainment waters.

Watching TV, you might have noticed Glen Campbell, Bill Medley, Bobby Hatfield and even the Righteous Brothers as regular guests on "Shindig," the "in" TV program that year. Shows like "Hullabaloo" tried to compete with it, but "Shindig" was the declared winner..

If you thought discos — real name, discotheques — were the result of a middle-age dream of returning to youth in the seventies, read on. "Memphis A-Go-Go" was written by Chuck Berry and recorded live in 1965 by Johnny Rivers, giving us the first hint of disco. The go-go fad originated at the Whiskey A-Go-Go, a Los Angeles night club that was part of a national chain and soon spread to radio station jingles and dance floors throughout North America and the world. The go-go fad also meant more than a bit of jingle in the jeans of Arthur Murray and heads of other dance studios, who had to keep up with the constant creativity and ingenuity of those who exercised on the disco dance floor.

1965

Johnny Rivers was a featured performer at the Whiskey A-Go-Go and we all enjoyed his show when he brought it to the Cave in 1966. Johnny was successful at more than disco, however. He was instrumental in launching the Fifth Dimension and songwriters Jimmy Webb and Laura Nyro. Some of his own hits included "Memphis," "Maybelline," "Mountain of Love," "The Seventh Show," "Poor Side of Town" (which he also wrote), "Secret Agent Man" and "Baby, I Need Your Love."

What were the Beatles doing at this time? They were busy churning out movies and they did an excellent job. *A Hard Day's Night* was followed by the equally successful *HELP!*, which featured "Ticket to Ride," written by John Lennon. The song was performed and filmed by the Beatles on alpine ski slopes and the scene was nothing short of terrific.

Where was Elvis? He was making movies, period. He sang "Dirty, Dirty Feeling" and "Put the Blame on Me" in a forgettable film called *Tickle Me*. Probably his worst film that year — or any year — was *Harem Scarem*, which in Britain was titled *Harem Holiday*. He also starred in *Frankie and Johnny*, *Paradise Hawaiian Style*, *Roustabout* and *Spin Out*. The movie *Paradise, Hawaiian Style* was a lackluster sequel to *Blue Hawaii*. These mundane movie plots didn't even please the most ardent Elvis fans.

The Beach Boys epitomized the growing surf sounds of the West Coast with "California Girls" and "Help Me, Rhonda" in 1965. For jazz buffs, Ramsey Lewis and his trio entered the pop scene with "The In-Crowd," written by Billy Page and originally released by Elvis Presley Music, Inc., and Rumbalero Music, Inc., in 1964. I mention this to point out the diversification of the Presley interests under the constant guidance of Colonel Tom Parker. Ramsey Lewis was very popular on the West Coast and in 1965, during one of his tours, he stopped in Vancouver long enough to thrill his fans at Isy's Supper Club.

The Elegant Parlour was the name of a rock 'n' roll nightclub of sorts in Vancouver. Little Daddy and the Bachelors were a musical group that frequently appeared there. That wouldn't be big news itself, except that Tommy Chong — of Cheech and Chong — ran the

1965

place. He later became part of Bobby Taylor and the Vancouvers in 1968. Somewhere along the way, Diana Ross, appearing in Vancouver with the Supremes, went clubbing, dropped into the Elegant Parlour, and heard the group. She contacted Berry Gordy, who immediately signed them. They flew to Detroit and cut a record, gaining local notoriety for their achievement. Shortly after, Cheech, an American draft dodger hiding out in Canada, met Chong, and they decided to form another rock band. They supplemented their shows with a unique brand of humor — and the rest is history. Cheech and Chong's movies are blockbusters and their humor, while appealing to a certain market, is well known. To prove that talent can be hereditary, it's worth noting that Tommy Chong's daughter starred in *Quest for Fire* and is herself a talent to be watched.

Vancouver has proven time and time again that it is a good town for preopening shows of all types. Mitzi Gaynor delighted audiences for over a decade by giving her dress performance in a pre-Las Vegas run at Vancouver's Cave Supper Club. It was at the Cave that Sammy Davis Jr., and his family appeared in the fifties as the Will Mastin Trio. Phyllis Diller, Diana Ross and the Supremes, Pat Boone, Frankie Laine, Bobbie Gentry, the Righteous Brothers, Chita Rivera, Wayne Newton, Anne Murray, Lena Horne, Johnny Rivers, the Everly Brothers, Count Basie and dozens more were spotlighted at the Cave, most of them with sold-out performances.

Because of the support and the love for these artists shown by the late Ken Stauffer, who owned the Cave, many of us in private radio were involved in years and years of publicizing and promoting the artists and their shows. In return, we got to meet and interview them in their more leisurely moments. Especially vivid memories include the time Diana Ross was going to redesign costumes for the show she and the Supremes were doing and Ken Stauffer volunteered Peggy (Keenan) Hodgins's sewing machine; the time Phyllis Diller needed shoes — she takes an exceptionally narrow size — and Peggy hired a car and squired her around; and the time Wayne Newton was accosted by a less-than-sober Vancouver newsman who accused him of being gay on tape and on camera to the dismay of a stunned media gathering at the Hotel Georgia in the midsixties. Former CKLG

1965

program director and hilarious morning man Roy Hennessy tells of attending the Bobbie Gentry press party on board a yacht hired for the day by the ingenious Ken Stauffer. Every man in the audience had admired Bobbie's figure, but her rear was spectacular. Roy claims he was completely chagrined when it shifted during the boat cruise and he realized that what you saw wasn't the real thing. No matter, says Roy, and I agree — "Ode to Billie Joe" revealed a remarkable talent.

In 1965, the entertainment industry experienced an incredible growth. At the same time the antiwar movement was burgeoning, creating a gulf between youth and the older generation as the "don't trust anyone over 30" feelings took hold. Rock 'n' roll was firmly entrenched — only the players were changing. And the man who had put it on the map, Elvis Presley, was wasting his talent in movies that didn't draw crowds.

There's not much more to be said about 1965 except that the Grammy Award for the best group of the year went to the Anita Kerr Singers for an album called *We Dig Mancini*. When you consider the plethora of talented groups and their albums that year, you have to wonder how this travesty occurred.

That was 1965.

Top Ten Hits

1. California Dreamin' — The Mamas and Papas
2. 96 Tears — ? and the Mysterians
3. What Becomes of the Broken-Hearted? — Jimmy Ruffin
4. Last Train to Clarksville — The Monkees
5. Reach Out, I'll Be There — The Four Tops
6. These Boots Are Made for Walking — Nancy Sinatra
7. Cherish — The Association
8. Strangers in the Night — Frank Sinatra
9. Kicks — Paul Revere and the Raiders
10. The Ballad of the Green Berets — Barry Sadler

Grammy Awards

Record of the Year	*"Strangers in the Night"* (Frank Sinatra)
Album of the Year	*A Man and His Music* (Frank Sinatra)
Song of the Year	*"A Man and a Woman"* (Anita Kerr Singers)
Best Male Vocalist	*Frank Sinatra* ("Strangers in the Night")
Best Female Vocalist	*Eydie Gorme* ("If He Walked into My Life")
Best Vocal Group	*Anita Kerr Singers* ("A Man and a Woman")

Top Movies

A Man for All Seasons
The Russians Are Coming, the Russians Are Coming
The Fortune Cookie
Blow-Up
Alfie
The Sand Pebble
A Man And a Woman
Georgy Girl
Hawaii

The Oscars

Best Picture	*A Man for All Seasons*
Best Director	Fred Zinneman (*A Man for All Seasons*)
Best Actor	Paul Scofield (*A Man for All Seasons*)
Best Actress	Elizabeth Taylor (*Who's Afraid of Virginia Woolf?*)
Best Supporting Actor	Walter Matthau (*The Fortune Cookie*)
Best Supporting Actress	Sandy Dennis (*Who's Afraid of Virginia Woolf?*)
Best Song	"Born Free" by John Barry and Don Black from *Born Free*

On Television

Hollywood Palace
Alfred Hitchcock
The Virginian
The Untouchables
Dean Martin Variety Show
My Three Sons
McHale's Navy
Tarzan
Roger Miller Variety Show
Peyton Place

Best Sellers

Valley of the Dolls
  Jacqueline Susann

The Fixer
  Bernard Malamud

In Cold Blood
  Truman Capote

With Kennedy
  Pierre Salinger

Death of a President
  William Manchester

The Embezzler
  Louis Auchincloss

Capable of Honor
  Allen Drury

On Broadway

Mame
Cabaret
Sweet Charity
I Do, I Do
The Killing of Sister George
Don't Drink the Water

1966

Rock 'n' roll came into adulthood in 1966, as did its original fans and the record buyers. What had begun in the fifties as a teenage fad still appealed to the same crowd — they were now just a little older.

The older crowd was lured into enjoying a form of rock 'n' roll by artists such as Herb Alpert and the Tijuana Brass, whose *Whipped Cream and Other Delights* and *Going Places* were number one and three, respectively, on the top-selling album list of the year.

The rock 'n' roll music of Bacharach and David as well as that of Beatles Lennon and McCartney was now being performed by pop artists, jazz singers and symphonies around the world. From Nancy Wilson to Frank Sinatra, everyone was singing this "youthful" music. It was heard everywhere, even on Muzak. (Has anyone anywhere ever actually claimed to enjoy Muzak?)

Frank Sinatra got a lot of attention in 1966. That forties vintage lady's man walked off with three Grammy Awards — two for the single "Strangers in the Night" and one for the album *A Man and His Music*.

At the same time, the drug scene was growing and many popular songs of 1966 reflected this trend. While Timothy Leary preached the "tune in, turn on" philosophy, musicians swiftly capitalized on the mood by writing music to go with it. Donovan's "Sunshine Superman" reflected the mushroom dope scene, as did "Eight Miles High" by the Byrds and "Along Comes Mary" by the Association.

A group whose sleepy, lyrical sounds evoked that stoned feeling was the Mamas and the Papas, led by John Phillips, with a string of hits that included "California Dreamin'," "Monday, Monday" and "I Saw Her Again Last Night." If the name sounds familiar to those who weren't around the pop scene of 1966, it's because Phillips reorganized the group in 1982 and replaced ex-wife Michelle with their daughter MacKenzie, who is better known for her role in "One Day at a Time."

As a result of the new, drug-inspired music, Canadian and American Top 40 radio stations began to censor rock music, eliminating lyrics or refusing to play the records that mentioned drugs. (Not all stations did this; some didn't care or perhaps simply

1966

didn't realize what was happening.) Record companies began putting the words of the record on the inside jacket so that program directors and music programmers could make a decision whether or not to play the record.

The British influence continued. Anything from Carnaby Street was chic, Mary Quant designer clothes and cosmetics were the rage, and James Bond and the Beatles were loved by just about everyone.

While the Beatles did not dominate the top portion of the charts in 1966, they still had some good hits — "Paperback Writer," "We Can Work It Out," "Yellow Submarine" and "Day Tripper."

For Simon and Garfunkel, "Homeward Bound" and "I Am a Rock" were popular, as was the recording of "Sounds of Silence." Other notable hits that year included the novelty song "Little Red Riding Hood" by Sam the Sham and the Pharoahs, "Painted Black" by the Rolling Stone and "Bus Stop" by the Hollies. The Stones also scored well with "19th Nervous Breakdown."

The first protest record of the era has been credited to Barry McGuire for "Eve of Destruction." The former member of the new Christy Minstrels penned this anthem of the sixties and then wrote the lyrics for "Hair," which was a Broadway blockbuster and later a movie.

Other protest songs were performed by Bob Dylan, Joan Baez and John Lennon. The emergence of protests through song, concerts and marches began to tell politicians that they did not have the support of the young in their war activities in Vietnam.

The "Batman" television show had been conceived, created and programmed for children. It quickly became a cult show for adults, however, and was so popular that business people stopped at their clubs and bars on the way home at night to unwind while watching the dynamic duo save Gotham City.

Don Adams had television audiences giggling with his preposterous impersonation of an undercover agent on "Get Smart." From that show came the popular expression "Sorry about that, Chief." Meanwhile, over on "Death Valley Days," another top-rated TV show, host Ronald Reagan resigned to campaign and become governor of California.

CKLG Deejay Paul Arthur with one of the Supremes.

Diana Ross with radio/TV personality Fred Latremouille.

Supremes press conference at Bayshore Inn.

Everyone loved Phyllis Diller, who wasn't really advertised on CKLG. She was a favorite then and still is today.

1966

The teen movie was quickly fading. Teenagers were no longer innocent enough to enjoy beach party flicks or Gidget-inspired personalities. The music and lyrics of the Beatles and the Rolling Stones had forever destroyed the naivety of previous generations of young people.

For Elvis Presley, the demise of teen movies was probably a blessing — he had three forgettable films produced in 1966: *Spinout*, *Easy Come, Easy Go* and *Double Trouble*. Even Roy Orbison starred in a box office disaster called *The Fastest Guitar Alive* — his first and last starring role. He had a cameo appearance, however, in the 1981 movie *Roadie*.

But 1966 did produce some good films. *The Russians Are Coming, the Russians Are Coming* was the funniest movie I saw that year. *Georgy Girl*, *Alfie*, *A Man and a Woman* and Stanley Kubrick's *2001: A Space Odyssey* were other standouts.

On the literary front, Jacqueline Susanne had astonishing success with *Valley of the Dolls*. Truman Capote also had a best seller in his chilling true-life account of a murder, *In Cold Blood*.

Here in Vancouver, I was busy at C-FUN and added another item to my agenda when, with Fred Latremouille, I cohosted the CBC half-hour network "Music Hop" television program which was broadcast across Canada. This program is worth mentioning because it is part of the Canadian radio-rock scene and because of some of the talent that went on to bigger and better things. Blake Emmons, who appeared on the show, has become a successful country singer and songwriter. Among other songs, he wrote "Help Me Make it to My Rockin' Chair" for B. J. Thomas. Terry Jacks and Susan Pesklevits (now best known as Susan Jacks) were regular entertainers on the show and went on to acclaim as "The Poppy Family." In March, 1970, they struck gold with "Which Way You Goin', Billy?" on London Records. "That's Where I Went Wrong," "Where Evil Grows" and "I Was Wondering" were other follow-up hits for the duo. Their last hit together appeared on the *Billboard* list in December 1971 — "No Good To Cry." Terry Jacks became an international star with "Seasons in the Sun" on Bell Records in January, 1974, which he credits me for playing first on CKWX. He also recorded "If You Go Away" and "Rock 'n' Roll" that same year. His 1983 hit was "You Fooled Me."

1966

Susan went solo and did well with "You're a Part of Me" in 1975 on the Mercury label. She continues to appear on variety shows in North America and has a reputation as an excellent entertainer. In 1982, she again hit the charts. Both of these young people were charming and easy to work with and it was a pleasure to see them make it to the top.

Tom Baird was the musical director of the show and he later went to work for Motown Records in Detroit. Tragically, Tom went sailing off the coast of San Diego one day and was never heard of again. We all miss him.

Thus, "Music Hop" not only entertained the country but also nurtured West Coast talent. As for Fred Latremouille, today he is the popular BCTV weatherman with anchor Tony Parsons on the Vancouver nightly news. In addition, he is at his and my old stomping ground C-FUN Radio as the morning man with veteran news personality and commentator J. J. Richards. I'll have to write another book to tell about the many personalities I have worked with over the years.

As December, 1966, drew to a close, you could turn on the radio and hear Frank Sinatra singing "That's Life," while daughter Nancy also topped the charts with "Sugar Town," a Lee Hazelwood tune. Paul Revere and the Raiders sang "Good Thing," Stevie Wonder's hit that month was "A Place in the Sun" and the Monkees had the number one weekly hit during the final days of 1966 with "I'm a Believer," written by Neil Diamond. The Monkees were a curious phenomenon, a carbon copy of the Beatles created by a television producer for a specific show. The New Vaudeville Band had a novelty hit with "Winchester Cathedral" and the Beach Boys were still feeling "Good Vibrations."

No description of 1966 would be complete without mentioning the fabulous Supremes headed by Diana Ross. They were the pride and joy of Berry Gordy's Detroit Motown Studios and certainly a welcome sight in Vancouver where they headlined at the Cave Supper Club. "You Keep Me Hangin' On," "My World Is Empty without You" and "Love Is Like an Itching in My Heart" were three of the Holland-Dozier-Holland numbers written for the glamorous trio.

1966

Phyllis Diller was a regular visitor to Vancouver and other places in Canada and she was a terrific personality to work with. When Peggy (Keenan) Hodgins put on a spray can filled with "Fresh Vancouver Air" as a CKLG promotion, Phyllis happily posed for pictures and took an air supply back to California.

Recently, I was asked by an interviewer if all the people mentioned in this book actually visited Vancouver. They certainly did. Vancouver was, and is, an important stop on the concert tour and in 1966 it helped many of today's superstars earn their success.

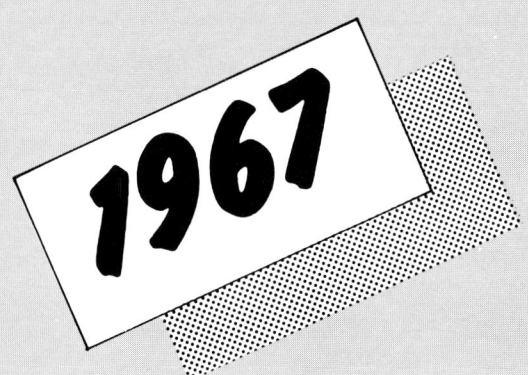

On Television

Batman
Ironside
Pat Boone
Mannix
The Flying Nun
Run for Your Life

Top Ten Hits

1. *To Sir with Love* — Lulu
2. *The Letter* — The Box Tops
3. *Ode to Billie Joe* — Bobbie Gentry
4. *Windy* — The Association
5. *I'm a Believer* — The Monkees
6. *Light My Fire* — The Doors
7. *Somethin' Stupid* — Frank and Nancy Sinatra
8. *Happy Together* — The Turtles
9. *Groovin'* — The Young Rascals
10. *Can't Take My Eyes Off of You* — Frankie Valli

Grammy Awards

Record of the Year	*"Up, Up and Away"* (Fifth Dimension)
Album of the Year	*Sgt. Pepper's Lonely Hearts Club Band* (The Beatles)
Song of the Year	*"Up, Up and Away"* (Jimmy Webb)
Best Male Vocalist	*Glen Campbell* ("By the Time I Get to Phoenix")
Best Female Vocalist	*Bobbie Gentry* ("Ode to Billie Joe")
Best Vocal Group	*Fifth Dimension* ("Up, Up and Away")

Top Movies

Bonnie and Clyde
The Graduate
In Cold Blood
Thoroughly Modern Millie
Camelot
The Dirty Dozen
Doctor Doolittle
Guess Who's Coming to Dinner?
Cool Hand Luke
Two for the Road
You Only Live Twice
Barefoot in the Park

The Oscars

Best Picture	*In the Heat of the Night*
Best Director	Mike Nichols (*The Graduate*)
Best Actor	Rod Steiger (*In the Heat of the Night*)
Best Actress	Katharine Hepburn (*Guess Who's Coming to Dinner?*)
Best Supporting Actor	George Kennedy (*Cool Hand Luke*)
Best Supporting Actress	Estelle Parsons (*Bonnie and Clyde*)
Best Song	"*Talk to the Animals*" by Leslie Bricusse from *Dr. Doolittle*

Best Sellers

Washington, D.C.
   Gore Vidal

The Medium Is the Massage
   Marshall McLuhan

Topaz
   Leon Uris

Why Are We in Vietnam?
   Norman Mailer

When She Was Good
   Phillip Roth
The Eighth Day
   Thornton Wilder

The New Industrial Scale
   John Kenneth Galbraith

On Broadway

Hello, Dolly
Ilya Darling
You Know I Can't Hear You When the Water's Running
How Now, Dow Jones
Sherry
The Homecoming

1967

The biggest show on earth in 1967 was the marriage of Elvis Presley to his protegé and girl friend, Priscilla Beaulieu. Although the wedding was highly publicized, the Las Vegas location was kept secret. If even a smattering of Presley's millions of fans had crashed the party, the Aladdin Hotel would have been wrecked.

Millions of female fans were crushed. As long as Elvis was single, they could always hope and dream that one day they might have a romance with him. For the time being, however, Elvis was married. Who could have predicted that this fairy tale romance would be dissolved by 1973?

Elvis's recording of "Guitar Man" moved up the charts but didn't make the Top 10 of the year; nor was his new album a sensational seller. And the movie he starred in that year — *Clambake* — was less than mediocre.

It appeared that Elvis Presley's popularity was waning. In 1967, he was upstaged by everyone from Frank Sinatra to Marvin Gaye and Englebert Humperdinck.

The 1967 Monterey Pop Festival brought the Haight-Ashbury scene in San Francisco into the limelight and added the word "hippie" to everyone's vocabulary. If you thought that Otis Redding was discovered "Sitting on the Dock of the Bay," you weren't far off. Otis was "discovered" at the Monterey Pop Festival, as was Janis Joplin. From this point on, Janis was one of the first ladies of rock. Her recording of Kris Kristofferson's composition "Me and Bobby McGee" remains the finest rendition of that song.

Janis was a complete change from the traditional female singers of the era, including Connie Francis, Diana Ross, Cher and Bobbie Gentry. Her tortured personal life was reflected in her singing. She represented the plain girl down the street who was bright and talented but never seemed to get it together. Her tragic drug-induced death in October, 1970, robbed the world of a great talent that never reached its potential.

The Monterey Festival is an important piece of rock history in North America. It was recorded on film and video cassette, showing the in-concert talents of Joan Baez, Bob Dylan, Judy Collins, Pete Seeger, Johnny Cash, Donovan, Peter, Paul and Mary and many

1967

more. It was also at this festival that Donovan introduced Canadian singer-composer Buffy Ste. Marie's composition "Universal Soldier" as "the song the BBC wouldn't let me play." Buffy's ability continues to be noted in the eighties. She and her partners, including Jack Nitzsche, won the 1982 Golden Globe Award and Academy Award for the best song, "Up Where We Belong."

The rock 'n' roll magazine *Rolling Stone* was born in 1967. Very shortly, this magazine joined *Cashbox* and *Billboard* as the "Bibles" of the industry.

Replacing the standard "elevator fare" of FM radio across North America was a new underground sound that revolutionized radio forever. With the discovery of FM's free-form capabilities, "stoned stereo" evolved as a reaction against the stifling programming formats on AM radio. The underground stations played long album cuts — most were unedited and contained many references to drugs and sex. FM radio became the voice of the hippies. To many of my generation, the message music, flower people and cults were something we could not understand.

There was an uneasy feeling in the air, a feeling captured previously in the 1965 hit "The Eve of Destruction" by Barry McGuire, which talked about Armageddon. Peter Fonda, Bruce Dern and Dennis Hopper starred in a psychedelic drug movie called *The Trip*, which was banned in the United States. If rock 'n' roll alienated the generations, this period scared hell out of everyone.

One of the most popular movies of 1967 was *The Graduate*, starring Dustin Hoffman, Anne Bancroft and Katherine Ross. It grossed $4 million in the first few weeks of its run and gave Simon and Garfunkel well-deserved recognition for their scoring of "The Sounds of Silence," "Scarborough Fair" and "Mrs. Robinson."

Another popular movie that year was *Bonnie and Clyde* which immortalized two ruthless outlaws, played by Warren Beatty and Faye Dunaway. The costumes in the movie appealed to the public and soon the Bonnie and Clyde look was everywhere as couples wore his-and-her outfits for work and play.

In 1967, *The Beatles' Magical Mystery Tour* was produced for BBC television in England and later released as a movie throughout the world. Both the album and the movie were huge successes. *The*

1967

Beatles' Magical Mystery Tour showed the diversity of the Beatles as they slowly changed their focus from love songs to mind trips and songs with a powerful message.

Also released in 1967, *Sgt. Pepper's Lonely Hearts Club Band* is a Beatles classic. It took 700 hours to produce in the studios. Today it sells to a new generation who didn't know the Beatles before they disbanded over a period of time from the end of 1969 to the beginning of 1970. It is difficult to be specific about when they disbanded because they had to record together for contractual reasons during 1969 and 1970. They split as a touring group during this time, however, to announce their individual careers.

When the Beatles returned from their soul-searching trip to India in 1967, they started yet another fad — Nehru shirts and jackets. George Harrison also began playing the sitar, bringing this ancient Indian instrument to the rock 'n' roll stage for the first time.

Charles Shultz was enjoying a large following with his *Peanuts* comic strip and one of the popular novelty songs of 1967 was "Snoopy versus the Red Baron" by the Royal Guardsmen. It sold a million copies in singles in just three weeks. Later, "The Return of the Red Baron," "Snoopy's Christmas" and, in 1968, "Snoopy for President" also sold well.

If one name stands out for durability, it is Herb Alpert and the Tijuana Brass. This clean-cut group with a flair for Mexican sounds had four spots on the best-seller list that year with *S.R.O.*, *Whipped Cream and Other Delights*, *Going Places* and *What Now My Love?* Today Herb Alpert continues to influence the music world as president of A & M Records which he founded with his pal Jerry Moss in 1962.

The Doors ("Light My Fire"), the Monkees ("I'm a Believer"), the Turtles ("Happy Together"), the Box Tops ("The Letter") and the Young Rascals ("Groovin' ") were making musical news that year. There were many other groups who liked starting their names with "the" also: the Seekers, whose rendition of "Georgy Girl" from the 1967 movie earned them prominence on the charts throughout the world, the Soul Survivors ("Expressway to Your Heart"), the Buckinghams ("Kind of a Drag"), the Strawberry Alarm Clock ("Incense and Peppermints"), the Music Explosion ("Little Bit o'

Bill Haley

1967

Soul"), the Esquires ("Get-on Up"), the Casinos ("Then You Can Tell Me Goodbye"), the Happenings ("I Got Rhythm"), the Temptations ("You're My Everything"), the Four Tops ("Bernadette"), the Grass Roots ("Let's Live for Today") and the Easybeats ("Friday on My Mind"). Of course, we can't ignore the Rolling Stones ("Ruby Tuesday") or the Supremes ("Love Is Here and Now You're Gone" and "The Happening") or the Fifth Dimension, whose "Up, Up and Away" was a happy song we heard being played everywhere we drove that year.

Although the "the" groups were certainly dominating the rock music picture, there were some lovely romantic songs popular in 1967 as well. One was the movie theme "Alfie," recorded by Dionne Warwick; another was "It Must Be Him," a hit for my friend Vicky Carr.

Vicky appeared many times in Vancouver — once at the Pacific National Exhibition in the Coliseum to a sell-out crowd and again during Timmy's Christmas Telethon, which I host each year — lately with my long-time friend Pat Boone. Paul Williams, Werner Klemperer, Robert Goulet, Shari Lewis and Patsy Gallant are others who have headlined this popular CBC yearly event.

"The Beat Goes On" kept Sonny and Cher before the public as they opened many star-studded concert tours throughout North America. But if the beat was going on for that successful team, it was becoming passé in the form of dancing. The new beats were different — complex and experimental.

Soul music held its own as an adjunct to the rhythm and blues part of the charts in 1967. Aretha Franklin had some success in the early sixties, but in 1967 she numbered in the Top 10 with "Respect." "Soul Man" by Sam and Dave was another song in that category.

In 1967, Neil Diamond had a hit with one of his own compositions, "Girl, You'll Be a Woman Soon." As a songwriter in the early sixties, he used to do one-night stands in Greenwich Village coffee houses, testing the water as a singer. Luck changed for him in 1965 when Jay and the Americans recorded a song Diamond had written — "Sunday and Me." In 1966, Diamond recorded "Solitary Man" and "Cherry, Cherry," which topped the charts in late 1966 and

1967

early 1967. Then in 1968 the Monkees recorded "I'm a Believer," which Diamond wrote for them along with "A Little Bit Me, A Little Bit You."

But it was in the early seventies that Diamond reached his potential when he scored the film *Jonathon Livingston Seagull*, which he also recorded for Columbia Records. It has since become the largest-selling original soundtrack in LP history. His relationship with Columbia Records is unique; he signed the largest deal in the company's history for future recordings.

Just when you think you have Neil Diamond pegged in a particular slot, he shows another side of his talent. Previously, if you mentioned *The Jazz Singer*, most people would think of Al Jolson. Mention *The Jazz Singer* today and everyone instantly thinks of Neil Diamond. Not only did he give a very credible performance as the star of the movie — especially for one who is not an actor — but the music he wrote and sang for the movie is one of the best movie scores ever written. Neither schmaltzy nor trendy, it appeals to teens as well as to men and women of all ages. We haven't heard the end of Neil Diamond's music yet.

Back in 1967, millions perched in front of their television sets every week at home, at work, in clubs and in lounges to watch the supersilliness of Rowan and Martin's "Laugh-In." Arte Johnson's portrayal of a German soldier was as ridiculous as "Hogan's Heroes" and Goldie Hawn had the world in love with her as she gyrated throughout the hour-long show. From a skit perfected by Judy Carne (the ex-Mrs. Burt Reynolds) came the expression "Sock It to Me," which later became the title of a song by Mitch Ryder and the Detroit Wheels.

Was it significant that one of the Beatles songs popular in 1967 was "Hello, Goodbye," a Lennon-McCartney composition? Some of the songs that played out the end of the year included "I Heard It through the Grapevine" by Gladys Knight and the Pips, "Chain of Fools" by Aretha Franklin, and "Woman, Woman" by the Union Gap. We didn't know it at the time, but the whole pop and rock picture was in a state of revolution.

Top Movies

2001: A Space Odyssey
Star!
Rosemary's Baby
Isadora
The Odd Couple
In Cold Blood

Top Ten Hits

1. Hey Jude — The Beatles
2. Love Is Blue — Paul Mauriat
3. Honey — Bobby Goldsboro
4. (Sittin' on) The Dock of the Bay — Otis Redding
5. People Got to Be Free — The Young Rascals
6. Sunshine of Your Love — Cream
7. This Guy's in Love with You — Herb Alpert
8. The Good, the Bad and the Ugly — Hugo Montenegro
9. Mrs. Robinson — Simon and Garfunkel
10. Tighten Up — Archie Bell and the Drells

Best Sellers

Myra Breckenridge
  Gore Vidal

Airport
  Arthur Hailey

The Salzburg Connection
  Helen McInness

Our Crowd
  Stephen Birmingham

The Naked Ape
  Desmond Morris

True Grit
  Charles Portis

The Instrument
  John O'Hara

House Made of Dawn
  M. Scott Momaday (Pulitzer Prize winner)

On Television

60 Minutes
The Man from U.N.C.L.E.
I Love Lucy
Rowan and Martin
The Doris Day Show
Merv Griffin

On Broadway

The Prime of Miss Jean Brodie
Plaza Suite
Hair
A Day in the Death of Joe Egg
The Great White Hope
George M.

The Oscars

Best Picture	*Oliver!*
Best Director	Carol Reed *(Oliver!)*
Best Actor	Cliff Robertson *(Charly)*
Best Actress	Katharine Hepburn *(The Lion in Winter)*
Best Supporting Actor	Jack Albertson *(The Subject Was Roses)*
Best Supporting Actress	Ruth Gordon *(Rosemary's Baby)*
Best Song	"The Windmills of Your Mind" by Michel Legrand, and Alan and Marilyn Bergman from *The Thomas Crown Affair*

Grammy Awards

Record of the Year	"Mrs. Robinson" (Simon and Garfunkel)
Album of the Year	*By the Time I Get to Phoenix* (Glen Campbell)
Song of the Year	"Little Green Apples" (Bobby Purcell)
Best Male Vocalist	*Jose Feliciano* ("Light my Fire")
Best Female Vocalist	*Dionne Warwick* ("Do you Know the Way to San Jose?")
Best Vocal Group	*Simon and Garfunkel* ("Mrs. Robinson")

1968

The Good, the Bad and the Ugly aptly summarizes the state of the world and its music in 1968. As the decade headed to a close, the times were changing rapidly — and, in some cases, nastily. Campus revolution raged throughout the western world. In the United States, the primary focus was the draft, the war in Vietnam and racism. This same mood of unrest also caused student protests for a variety of reasons in France, West Germany, Poland, Czechoslovakia and Japan. In sympathy, a few demonstrations occurred in Canada, but the unrest was not as acute in this country as it was elsewhere.

The assassinations of Dr. Martin Luther King and Senator Robert F. Kennedy in April and June, respectively, of that year were cruel demonstrations of the political and social problems in North America. Scores of publications have documented these tragedies and the effect felt everywhere. Certainly the death of Dr. Martin Luther King underscored the need for an end to racism. From this tragedy came the song "Abraham, Martin and John," composed by Dick Holler and sung by Dion in his 1968 comeback.

The changes in the music business scared the hell out of deejays of my generation — we simply didn't understand this new music. The sounds ranged from screaming, screeching psychedelic rock 'n' roll to the very gentle "This Guy's in Love with You," written by Hal David and Burt Bacharach and brought to the Hit Parade by Herb Alpert.

The Beatles still had a tremendous impact on the recording and entertainment world, but they were slowly fading as each of the four personalities began to go his own separate way. John Lennon and Paul McCartney wrote "Eleanor Rigby" and to this day everyone has his own interpretation of the song. This amused the Beatles, of course, and they were quoted by several sources with different explanations of this recording.

"Eleanor Rigby" figured in the top songs of the year, but not in the Top 10 — "Hey Jude" captured a spot in that list. Another Lennon-McCartney effort, it touched a nerve and became a classic akin to the singalongs of the fifties. One of the Beatles' business advisors later recalled that Paul McCartney wrote "Hey Jude" to cheer Julian Lennon up during the trauma of his parents' breakup over Yoko

1968

Ono. The song was originally called "Hey Julian," but the title didn't have that certain "ring" to it and was changed to "Hey Jude."

Country singer Johnny Cash was by now on a major comeback after a very chaotic career. His recording of "Folsom Prison Blues," a single on the album of the same name, was an expression of the down-home roots of North America. Johnny later told me that this record was an important part of his rejuvenation as he struggled with his drug and alcohol problems. Johnny Cash is simply one of the finest gentlemen I have ever had the pleasure of working with. His world-class status as a country singer today is well deserved.

When Jimmy Webb wrote "MacArthur Park" he had a lasting effect on the recording industry and the broadcasting business. The original recording of the song as sung by British actor and *Camelot* star Richard Harris played for a solid seven minutes. Record producers were amazed and modern-day announcers thrilled. Today seven-minute recordings are reasonably common — particularly on FM radio stations — but in those days anything even a few seconds over three minutes was simply not played. By this time, "boss" radio had tightened up, toughened up and shut up the personality of the deejays. Top 40 radio was a cloning system — you could travel anywhere and be assured that the rock station you preferred in your home town (if it was large enough) would be duplicated anywhere you went in North America. "MacArthur Park" was a subtle indication of the wave of change that was happening in the late sixties. Two-minute recording cuts were disappearing — it was a time for experimentation and creative expression. But it was also a time for a clear definition of AM and FM radio. AM became tighter, with less emphasis on personality while FM deejays were permitted — encouraged, in fact — to express themselves and develop what would rapidly become known as underground radio. Because of its overwhelming success, "MacArthur Park" was aired on both AM and FM radio and, therefore, set a precedent for other recordings that joined the pop, acid and underground rock genres.

I always enjoyed working with Bobby Goldsboro and his rendition of the Bobby Russell song "Honey" was both pretty and romantic. Other songs that fit into the "pretty" category that year included another Bobby Russell tune, "Little Green Apples," which

Backstage with Tom Jones at the Queen Elizabeth Theatre, Vancouver, 1979.

*Interviewing Tony Bennett,
Vancouver, 1978.*

1968

Bobbie Gentry performed at the Cave Supper Club to the delight of the Vancouver audience, myself included. Everyone adored Bobbie Gentry. I hope one day she'll make a return to the recording business. Another pretty song that year was "The Windmills of your Mind," composed by that brilliant French musician Michel Legrand, with lyrics by the successful Hollywood team Alan and Marilyn Bergman, who have worked on dozens of movie scores, including Barbra Streisand's *A Star is Born* in the seventies and *Tootsie* in the eighties.

Simon and Garfunkel captured two Grammy Awards in 1968 for "Mrs. Robinson" and "Scarborough Fair." The latter had been written in 1966, but it didn't make the Top 100 until 1968.

For *Playboy* readers, cartoonist and social commentator Shel Silverstein is synonymous with giggles, guffaws and hoots. But for the Irish Rovers, a transplanted group of Irish-Canadians, Shel Silverstein meant a strong and healthy bank balance in 1968 when this nationally adored group recorded Silverstein's composition "The Unicorn."

When Tom Jones comes on stage, normally reticent matrons start swooning and screaming. Tom Jones belongs to a unique club of three members. The other two members are Frank Sinatra and Elvis Presley. They are the only three teen idols who later became stars appealing to adults — both male and female. Sinatra achieved this evolution in the forties, Presley in the fifties and Jones in the sixties — 1968 to be exact. No other entertainer has ever joined this group.

Macho and sexy with an animal magnetism describes Tom Jones. He was a white blues singer whose phrasing and cadence convinced those who had never seen him that he must be black. Born in Wales, with that same appeal that makes women act like groupies around Richard Burton, Jones was playing gigs as Tommy Scott and the Senators. In 1964, musician and recording executive Gordon Mills, who had written "It's Not Unusual," met Jones and began managing him. The first thing Mills did was to capitalize on the movie *Tom Jones* that was rollicking its way around the world. Later Jones recorded "Little Lonely One," "What's New Pussycat," "With These Hands," "Thunderball," "Green, Green Grass of Home," "Delilah" and the list goes on. He had toured North America before 1968, but it wasn't until that year that he dropped his act geared toward teenagers and began concentrating on a middle-of-the-road audience. Since then, he has been charming people — mainly women — over 30. A regular visitor to Vancouver, he's known for his love of fishing, fine wine, good food and the good life in general. In the early 1980s he gained local attention by squiring Brooke Shields to a few of Vancouver's finer night spots.

Joining Tom Jones as a sexy singer in person and on television sets around the world was Arnold George Dorsey (also known as Gerry Dorsey). Once again, Gordon Mills struck gold, suggesting that Dorsey change his name to Englebert Humperdinck. Born in India, Englebert Humperdinck began his show business career in England. His hits included "There Goes My Everything," "The Last Waltz," "A Man without Love," "Am I That Easy to Forget?" and "Release Me," which is his signature. Today he continues to do a few concert tours, plays Las Vegas and has joined other stars, including Canada's Anne Murray, for television specials.

The British contingent as managed by Gordon Mills didn't begin and end with Tom Jones and Englebert Humperdinck. Gilbert O'Sullivan was another singer Mills groomed. His hits included "Alone Again" and "Clair." He never reached the sensational status of his two colleagues, but he did respectably on the charts around the world.

The rock opera *Tommy* began as a British television production in 1968. Peter Townshend wrote the book, lyrics and music for this rock opera, to which his pals, the other members of the Who, contributed some numbers as well. *Tommy* eventually sold over 10 million copies (at last count) as an album and was performed by the Who at the London Coliseum in 1969 and at the Metropolitan Opera House in New York in 1970. Roger Daltry and other members of the Who had major parts in the movie version, which also starred Ann Margret and Oliver Reed and included a cameo appearance by Elton John as the pinball wizard.

While many termed San Francisco "the Liverpool of the West" in the 1960s, it was also both the starting and the stopping point for many groups, including the Charlatans, the Grateful Dead, Country Joe and the Fish, the Chocolate Watchband, Quicksilver Messenger Service, Moby Grape and the Heavenly Blues Band. Remember any of them?

Glen Campbell returned to Vancouver as a superstar in 1979.

By 1979 Rick Nelson had grown up to be a handsome singer. Too much Hollywood and too little ambition stopped him from being the star he could have been.

With Prime Minister Trudeau at outdoor rally in Vancouver, 1977.

Johnny Cash returns to Vancouver in 1979.

1968

The Jefferson Airplane, a San Francisco group, had a few aborted take-offs but eventually got into the air with Grace Slick as lead singer. Grace was not yet able to command the spotlight by herself — she was up against Janis Joplin, a formidable talent whom *Cashbox* called "a kind of mixture of Leadbelly, a steam engine, Calamity Jane, Bessie Smith, an oil derrick, and rot gut bourbon. . . ."

In 1968, Credence Clearwater Revival emerged from San Francisco. The group's leader, Jim Fogerty, wrote "Proud Mary," which shot the band to the top of the record polls across North America. The group followed this with a dozen hit recordings of Fogerty's own compositions, which included "Bad Moon Rising," "Lodi," "Green River," "Up Around the Bend" and "Looking Out My Back Door." I must admit to a bit of prejudice here — Credence Clearwater Revival is one of my favorite groups of the past few years.

The big entertainment story of the year was Elvis Presley's comeback. One day he wandered down the street in Los Angeles and discovered, to his dismay, that no one recognized him. Elvis was so shocked that in June 1968 he began taping a Christmas special, which was aired on Thursday, December 3. As millions of North Americans sat riveted to their television sets, Elvis headlined his first-ever TV special.

Fans in the audience thrilled to a nostalgic medley of his first hits, including "Heartbreak Hotel" and "Hound Dog." My "agents" reported to me that even the television studio was electrified by the taping. The show was one of my favorite Elvis performances ever.

Elvis was back. In person, on television and through recordings, Elvis was back in the most spectacular comeback ever staged. He managed to maintain the momentum from that year right up until his tragic death in 1977.

For followers of Joe South, 1968 marked the year he won two Grammies for the song "Games People Play." That title had surfaced first as a popular self-help book and then as a movie. Joe was another entertainer who headlined the Cave Supper Club.

The Cave had opened the year with Frankie Laine. Frankie had a rebirth of hits in the late sixties. He had taken Marty Robbins's composition of "Lord, You Gave Me a Mountain" and placed himself back on the charts after an absence of more than a decade.

1968

Remember, by 1968 Frankie Laine had been around 20 years — his first big hit was "That's My Desire," which surfaced in 1947. Frankie is still around today, appearing in concerts and on television and doing commercials — the guy certainly has staying power.

We all trooped to the Cave to enjoy a variety of acts each year and 1968 was no different. Eric Burdon and the Animals, the Nitty Gritty Dirt Band and Harper's Bazarre were just a handful of the popular sellout groups that graced the stage. Rock acts were now acceptable in a nightclub setting. As the supper club business began to die, club owners began booking contemporary acts that would fill the house. Eric Burdon's recording of "House of the Rising Sun" blew just about every fuse in the club. (It was a remake of a song that had been around for a while and had shot Joan Baez into the limelight in the early sixties.) The Simon and Garfunkel composition "59th Street Bridge Song," performed by Harper's Bazarre, was a more acceptable ballad for a nightclub setting. Ed Ames, the Righteous Brothers, Bill Medley and Bobby Hatfield were always popular with Vancouver audiences. One performer termed the Righteous Brothers' brand of blues "blue-eyed soul."

The Cave's billboard in May of 1968 included two other great names — Eartha Kitt and my old friend Bobby Darin. In addition, Jimmie Rodgers made an appearance at the Cave — his first after a bad automobile accident.

Back in the late fifties, Kenny Rogers had played a small, intimate Vancouver club called the Arctic Club and didn't draw much of a crowd at all. The reason could be that the Arctic Club appealed to the soft jazz set. Among the singers who graced the ministage were Pat Suzuki and Rolf Harris. In 1968, however, Kenny Rogers and the First Edition were the headliners at the Cave and did very well. Their hits included "Ruby, Don't Take Your Love To Town" and "Rueben James." The First Edition was organized by several members of the New Christy Minstrels. There was a long empty period, which Rogers cheerfully talks about today, between his First Edition hits and his present hits. Kenny Rogers is now a firmly established star and he has also done well in the movies.

Another group that appeared at the Cave in 1968 was the Fifth Dimension, which sang its hits "Up, Up and Away" and "The

Roy Orbison in Vancouver again.

1968

Wedding Bell Blues." Following that group were the Righteous Brothers (again to a sellout crowd) and Chuck Berry, whom I had met in the fifties. Chuck is the daddy of rock 'n' roll and his infectious music still gets dedicated rock 'n' rollers moving today.

By the end of 1968, we had seen Richard M. Nixon elected the thirty-seventh president of the United States and Jacqueline Kennedy marry Aristotle Onassis in a small but well-publicized wedding in Greece. Yale University had announced it would admit women for the first time in its 267-year history.

Should I admit that my favorite song that year was "Mrs. Robinson" by Simon and Garfunkel? Or would you believe that it was "Honey" by my old chum Bobby Goldsboro? In any case, it was a very good year for music, and the Beatles' recording of "Hey Jude" highlighted the year as one of the most all-encompassing songs they ever produced

1969

On Television

The Bold Ones
Name of the Game
Hogan's Heroes
David Frost
Room 222

Top Ten Hits

1. *Sugar, Sugar* — The Archies
2. *Aquarius/Let the Sunshine In* — The Fifth Dimension
3. *I Can't Get Next to You* — The Temptations
4. *Honky Tonk Woman* — The Rolling Stones
5. *Everyday Woman* — Sly and the Family Stone
6. *Dizzy* — Tommy Roe
7. *Hot Fun in the Summertime* — Sly and the Family Stone
8. *I'll Never Fall in Love Again* — Tom Jones
9. *Build Me a Buttercup* — The Foundations
10. *Crimson and Clover* — Tommy James and the Shondells

Grammy Awards

Record of the Year — *"Aquarius/Let the Sunshine In"* (The Fifth Dimension)
Album of the Year — *Blood, Sweat and Tears* (Blood, Sweat and Tears)
Song of the Year — *"Games People Play"* (Joe South)
Best Male Vocalist — *Harry Nilsson* ("Everybody's Talkin'")
Best Female Vocalist — *Peggy Lee* ("Is That all There Is?")
Best Vocal Group — *The Fifth Dimension* ("Aquarius/Let the Sunshine In")

Top Movies

Anne of the Thousand Days
Butch Cassidy and the Sundance Kid
Hello, Dolly!
Z
Alice's Restaurant
They Shoot Horses, Don't They?
The Sterile Cuckoo
Midnight Cowboy
Bob & Carol & Ted & Alice

The Oscars

Best Picture	*Midnight Cowboy*
Best Director	*John Schlesinger* (Midnight Cowboy)
Best Actor	Maggie Smith *(The Prime of Miss Jean Brodie)*
Best Actress	John Wayne *(True Grit)*
Best Supporting Actor	Gig Young *(They Shoot Horses, Don't They?)*
Best Supporting Actress	Goldie Hawn *(Cactus Flower)*
Best Song	*"Raindrops Keep Fallin' on My Head"* by Burt Bacharach and Hal David from *Butch Cassidy and the Sundance Kid*

On Broadway

Hello, Dolly!
The Fantasticks
Mame
Man of La Mancha
Fiddler on the Roof
The Boys in the Band
The Great White Hope

Best Sellers

Ada
    Vladimir Nabokov

The Godfather
    Mario Puzo

The Love Machine
    Jacqueline Susanne

Portnoy's Complaint
    Philip Roth

Slaughterhouse-Five
    Kurt Vonnegut, Jr.

The Peter Principle
    Dr. Laurence J. Peter and Raymond Hall

1969

From the Sea of Tranquility, astronaut Neil Armstrong reported, "It's big and bright and beautiful." In the summer of 1969, Armstrong and Buzz Aldrin became the first men to land on the moon. The whole world watched as the most spectacular television program ever produced was beamed to us courtesy of the American taxpayers.

It may have been a sea of tranquility on the moon, but here on earth change was still in the air and the world of music reflected it. The musical *Hair* had opened on Broadway in 1968 with little fanfare. By 1969, however, it was a full-fledged hit. It gave us a batch of beautiful songs, including "Aquarius," "Hair" and "Let the Sunshine In." *Hair* expressed the sense of optimism and rebirth that people felt as changes took place in our attitudes, mores and lifestyles. I doubt that any song was played more than "Aquarius" in 1969 and certainly we all knew the phrase, "This is the dawning of the age of Aquarius." No, it wasn't rock in its original formula — far from it — but it was a rock opera, a contemporary musical that appealed to all ages. Once again, music had provided a bridge to help close the gap between rebellious teenagers and their bewildered parents.

Two major events in 1969 showed the good and the bad sides of rock concerts, or any event where massive crowds are gathered. The Woodstock Music and Art Fair, held in August 1969 near Bethel, New York, drew an estimated 400,000 people. The take on the gate alone was in excess of $500,000. Advertised as a "peace, love and rock" event, the three-day festival included such headliners as Joan Baez, the Jefferson Airplane, Sly and the Family Stone, Jimi Hendrix, the Who, Led Zeppelin and Janis Joplin. Woodstock was unique for its nonviolence. Well-organized and unusually well behaved crowds joined together in an event that will probably never be repeated. The Woodstock Festival was the definitive rock statement of 1969.

In contrast, the Altamont Concert, staged free by the Rolling Stones in December, 1969, was chaotic and violent. The appearance of the Hell's Angels, who were allegedly hired as bodyguards, turned the concert into a brutal fighting match that resulted in death and injury. This tragic turn of events did nothing for rock 'n' roll and was certainly detrimental to the Rolling Stones. They did not appear again in the United States for another 18 months.

Like many groups, the Rolling Stones had problems with

1969

drugs. There were many rumors when Brian Jones left the Stones in 1969. There were even more rumors when, within 24 days of his leaving, he was found face down in the pool of his English mansion — he allegedly died from a drug overdose. If anything positive could be said about the Rolling Stones that year, it was that Mick Jagger and Marianne Faithful were keeping gossip columnists busy following the soap-opera events of their romance.

John Lennon and Yoko Ono staged a more intimate event that year — they held a love-in at the King Edward Hotel in Toronto. It was really almost a nonevent. The couple stayed in bed and entertained the press at a conference as they celebrated their new-found love and called for world peace. This was Lennon's emergence as a philosopher.

Before their love-in, John and Yoko stayed at the ranch belonging to Rompin' Ronnie Hawkins, long one of Canada's leading rock 'n' roll bad guys. Ronnie had always been a character and his relationship with Lennon is curious. Canada's charismatic Prime Minister Pierre Trudeau also got into the act when he formally welcomed John and Yoko to Canada as he has welcomed many rock stars. His estranged wife, Margaret, apparently shares Trudeau's affinity for rock stars. At one point she was reported AWOL with the Rolling Stones. You can read her books to get the full story.

If you check the Top 10 for 1969, you'll see that the Beatles weren't there. Nevertheless, Lennon and his fellow Beatles had a hit that year with "Get Back" from the album *Let It Be*. Meanwhile, there were conflicting reports about the breakup of the Beatles, which finally took place in 1970. Throughout July and August of 1969, the four were busily recording together at the Abbey Road Studio in London. According to Beatles watchers, they actually went out and climbed onto the roof during one segment of filming and entertained passersby. This, then, would be their last unofficial public appearance.

No review of 1969 would be complete without mentioning the second phase of the women's movement, which had begun in the early sixties with Betty Friedan and which continued to gain momentum with Kate Millett and Gloria Steinem. Abandoning her sex kitten image, Jane Fonda became an important figure in the move-

Charlie Rich, Vancouver Coliseum, 1974.

With Chief Dan George in Vancouver.

Cliff Richard in Vancouver.

(courtesy Valerie Giles)

Elvis in Seattle, Washington, 1976.

Jack Cullen, Red, Vic Waters and Gene Kern.

Double platinum record presented to Red Robinson by RCA in 1978 for sale of 200,000 units of "Elvis — A Canadian Tribute" which Red narrated. World-wide sales to date have exceeded 600,000 units sold.

Fiesty BCTV hotliner Jack Webster, Peggy (Keenan) Hodgins, Jack Cullen. Vancouver Media Club.

Red hosts Annual CBC Timmy Telethon with Shari Lewis for B.C. Lions Society for Crippled Children.

1969

ment, combining both feminism and political activism with her movie career. It is probably no accident that two of the top hits of 1969 were "Honky Tonk Woman" by the Rolling Stones and "Everyday Woman" by Sly and the Family Stone. It was the year of the woman.

Hoyt Axton's mother, Mae Axton, had written many songs for Elvis Presley — including his original hit, "Heartbreak Hotel" — and in 1969 Hoyt himself wrote a winner, "Joy to the World," which the Three Dog Night recorded. If you ever wondered how Three Dog Night got its name, you can ask Rolf Harris or someone from Qantas Airlines. They will tell you that in the Australian outback a three-dog night is a cold night when you need at least three dogs to keep you warm.

David Clayton Thomas joined the group Blood, Sweat and Tears and their blockbuster recording of "Spinning Wheel" still goes around today. It took the continent by storm, as did several other hits of theirs. At the Grammy Awards in 1969, they walked off with several awards, including one for best album of the year and another for their performance of "Variations on a Theme by Eric Satie." Other Blood, Sweat and Tears hits included "You've Made Me So Very Happy," "And When I Die" and "Lucretia Mae Evil."

When Johnny Cash won the Country Music Award for 1969, everyone was thrilled. But no one believed he earned it solely for his rendition of "A Boy Named Sue." Johnny had piled up hit after hit after hit. Today he is still a star.

Country music was going uptown and reaching into the mainstream. Glen Campbell will tell you that 1969 was one of his better years. His smash hit "Galveston" was in good company as pop-country drew an entirely new listening audience to the Top 40.

Some singers sprint to the top almost by accident. One such performer was B. J. Thomas, who has a very soft voice. B. J. sang "Raindrops Keep Fallin' on My Head," a Bacharach-David number featured in *Butch Cassidy and the Sundance Kid*. If you happen to see that movie on your video machine or on TV, you'll realize that there was no story line for that song in the movie. Still, there is hardly a woman in the world who didn't enjoy seeing Paul Newman acting silly on a bicycle and the musical score of the movie was superb. For B. J. Thomas, it was his biggest taste of stardom. Today he continues to record country songs.

1969

Other songs we watched being lip-synced on television — one of the great tragedies of entertainment — were "Hurt So Bad" by the Lettermen and "I'll Never Fall in Love Again" by Dionne Warwick, another in her barrage of Bacharach and David hits. "Wedding Bell Blues" (The Fifth Dimension), "Proud Mary" (Credence Clearwater), "Games People Play" (Joe South), "Leaving on a Jet Plane" (Peter, Paul and Mary), "Come Saturday Morning" (the Sandpipers) and "Lay, Lady, Lay" (Bob Dylan) were others that caught our attention in 1969. Poet Rod McKuen has produced some beautiful work over the years, but "Jean," the song he wrote for the movie *The Prime of Miss Jean Brodie*, is probably his best-known number.

In 1969, Sammy Davis Jr. wrote a book called *Yes, I Can*, which describes his fight to the top of the show biz ladder. Some of that fight took place in Vancouver when Sammy and his father and uncle appeared as the Will Mastin Trio at the Cave Supper Club.

Flipping through my scrapbooks I note that Tony Bennett, Mitzi Gaynor, Louis Prima, Sheila McRae, O. C. Smith, Connie Stevens, the Mills Brothers, Ella Fitzgerald, Bill Medley, Al Martino, Little Richard, Paul Anka, Damita Jo (with comedian Peter Legge, now the publisher of *TV Week*), Sonny and Cher, the Righteous Brothers, Trini Lopez, Phyllis Diller, Anthony Newley, Pete Barbutti (with Judy and Jim Ginn) and the New Vaudeville Band all headlined at the Cave Supper Club. Vancouver provides top-notch entertainment and 1969 was an exceptionally fine year.

As for me, by 1969 I had switched roles and was becoming more involved in the management end of broadcasting at CJOR. The generation gap had finally zapped me. The original rock 'n' roller with memories firmly entrenched in Nashville and Memphis had matured into a husband and a father. Nevertheless, I continued to meet and to greet the stars visiting the station, attended dozens of concerts and traveled to Las Vegas to catch the shows of the day. Then, following a stint at CKLG as an account executive, I was approached by my alma mater, CKWX, to do the morning slot, where I am today after 10 years. In the station's 60 years of existence, I have been the longest-running morning man.

The era of rock 'n' roll was an exciting time. As rock 'n' roll makes a comeback in the eighties, I realize that my youthful judgment

1969

wasn't wrong after all. That music can hold its own anywhere, anytime.

Today my teenage children turn on the radio and listen to the rockabilly strains of groups like the Stray Cats. To them it's a whole new sound, but to me and my generation it's rockabilly music from the beginning. Rock 'n' roll has come full circle. And the beat goes on.

Dedication

To everyone, everywhere, who has ever experienced the joy of working in radio (and television) and especially to the guys who made the golden era of the deejays what it was — George "Hound Dog" Lorenz, Al Jarvis, Alan Freed, Tommy Edwards, Bill Ballance, Gil Henry, William B. Williams, B. Mitchell Reid, and a host of others. They were there at the dawning of rock 'n' roll, the pied pipers of the genre, and expanded musical horizons throughout North America.

Photo Credits

Peter Battistoni
Craig Hodge
John Helcermanas
Campbell Studios
Brian Thompson
Rolly Ford
Photo Art Commercial (Portland Oregon)
Barbara Dobie
John Gregory
Peggy Keenan Hodgins
Valerie M.E. Giles
Leslie Mister
Henry Tregillas

Glossary

Benny's Overcoats — Cashmere, half-length coats with padded shoulders. Good quality, but not a classic, enduring style. Warm, though.

Cherry Coke — Good old Coca-Cola with a shot of cherry syrup served at soda fountains. Delicious.

Cool — The "In" state that everyone hoped he or she expressed.

Cover Record — When a "Negro" (now known as a black) entertainer recorded a best-selling number, a white entertainer would "cover" the same song so the recording could be aired on traditionally white radio stations. An example is "Shake, Rattle and Roll," which was originally recorded by Joe Turner and later made popular by Bill Haley and the Comets and Elvis Presley.

Disc Jockey/Deejay/DJ — A word coined in the early fifties referring to the job of the announcer, which was to "ride the records" and watch the visual volume indicator to make sure the needle didn't go into the red area on the controls and cause distortion to the sound. (Relate this to your own simple recording equipment when you get a high treble or low bass sound.)

D.A. — Duck's Ass haircut for met, popular in the fifties. (See a duck if your barber can't explain.)

Evening in Paris — The first bottle of perfume most young North American girls ever bought. Very few of them continued to use it after they graduated from high school.

Hot Rods — Customized cars that allowed teens to realize their fantasies. When the car people in Detroit caught on, they started manufacturing cars to the specifications innovated by ambitious teenagers.

The Most	Something that was great.
Motorcycle Jackets	Still popular today, these leather jackets originated in the fifties. Popularized by Elvis Presley, Sal Mineo, and Marlon Brando, among others, as well as by the movies *Blackboard Jungle* and *On the Waterfront*. Today's Fonzie from "Happy Days" on TV continues the trend.
Penny Loafers	Semihip high school "in" girls and boys, or guys and gals, as they were called then, wore these sturdy, no-nonsense plain brown (or white) loafers with a space at the top to stuff a penny in for good luck.
Rock 'n' Roll/Rock and Roll	New "youth" or "teen" music introduced by Alan Freed.
Sock Hops	School dances held in the gym or hallways in the fifties. (You didn't wear shoes in the gym!) Jiving to rock 'n' roll music was also easier with socks or ballerina flatties.
Strides/Chinos/ Drapes	Men's — and occasionally women's — pants that were normally charcoal grey or black (worn with pink shirts) and had tight 14-inch ankles ballooning into 33-inch knees. Some featured a five-button waist. Elvis wore these with his famous gold lamé jacket.
Zoot Suiters	Guys who wore all the trendy clothes, including strides.

Index

Abbey Road Studios 217
A and M Records 197
Abbotsford Airport 21,122
Ackery, Ivan 32,33
Adams, Don 187
Aldred, David 53
American Bandstand 53,78,79, 94, 104,108,126,146
Ames Brothers 146
Aldrin, Buzz 216
Alpert, Herb 186,197,202
Allen, Gene 169
Allison, Jerry (see Crickets) 142
Altamont Concert 216
Andrew Sisters 10
Arthur, Paul 189
ATCO Records 173
Ames, Ed 211
Angels, The 139
Animals, The 169
Anita Kerr Singers 183
Anka, Paul 7,44,49,52,53,101,104, 108,109,152,172,175
Arctic Club 211
Armstrong, Louis 29
Armstrong, Neil 216
Arnold, Eddy 123
Association, The 186
Avalon, Frankie 46,53,104
Axton, Hoyt 33,220
Axton, Mae 33,220

Bacharach, Burt (see also Bacharach and David) 123,147,172, 186,202,220,221
Baez, Joan 59,169,187,194,211,216
Baird, Tom 190
Baker, Laverne 29
Balance, Bill 86
Ball, Kenny 126
Bancroft, Anne 195
Barber, Chris 126
Barbotti, Pete 221
Bare, Bobby 109,151
Barrett, Pat 32
Basie, Count 29,182
"Batman" TV Series 187
B.C. Lions Society for Crippled Children 219
Beach Boys 14,29,127,138,153,176, 179,180,181,190
Beatles, The 14,29,32,84,104,105, 122,123,138,153,156,157,158,160, 161,165,166,167,172,178,181, 186,187,190,195,199,202,213,217
Beatty, Warren 195
Beaulieu, Pricilla 194
Belafonte, Harry 23,45,126,146
Berman, Shelly 109
Bennett, Tony 146,221
Bergman, Alan and Marilyn 206
Bernstein, Leonard 119
Berry, Chuck 6,14,15,20,29,131, 138,180,213
Big Bopper, The (see also J.P. Richardson) 18,49
Billboard 161
Bilk, Acker 126
Black, Bill 65
"Blackboard Jungle, The" Movie 19
Blackwell, Bumps 48
Blood, Sweat and Tears 220
Blore, Chuch 86
Bobbettes, The 139
Boliska, Al 134,135
Bond, James 187
Bono, Sonny 173
Boone, Daniel 130

Boone, Debbie 131
Boone, Pat 7,11,83,130,131,134, 151,152,182,198
Boone, Shirley 131
Boss Radio 179
Boston Pops 178
Bowen, Jimmy 49,53
Brewer, Teresa 23
Brown Myra 78
Brando, Marlon 19,36,131
Brothers Four, The (see also Dick Foley) 100
Brooks, Donnie 143
Brown, Roy 143
Brubeck, Dave 100
Brubeck Quartet, The Dave 100
Buckinghams 197
Burgess, Dave 75
Burdon, Eric 169
Burlison, Paul 143
Burnette, Dorsey 143
Burnette, Johnny 143
Burns, Carl 94
Burton, Richard 206
Byrds, The 178,186

Caesar and Cleo 173
Calypso 23,45,53,126
Campbell, Glen 75,180,220
Canadaires, The 32
Cannon, Freddie 79,101
Capitol Theatre 32,33
Capitol Records 18,57,87,156
Captain and Tenille, The 118
Capote, Truman 142,189
Carnaby Street 187
Carne, Judy 199
Carr, Vicky 198
Carson, Johnny 53,152
Carter, Mel 146
Cash, Johnny 101,108,194,203,220
Casinos 198
Cave Supperclub 181,182,190,206, 210,211,221
CBC (Canadian Broadcasting Corporation) 22,189
CBS 86
C-FUN Radio 147,150,153,156,157, 161,164,165,174,175,176,189
CJOR Radio 11,21,22,221
Chacksfield, Frank 9
Chad and Jeremy 169
Champs, The 75
Chanel, Bruce 127
Chancellor Records 53
Charlatans, The 207
Charms, The 11
Charles, Ray 13,130,138
Checker, Chubby 109,115,126,143, 146,174
Cheech and Chong 181,182
Cheers, The 18
Cher 173,194
Chess Records 14
Chief Dan George 218
Chiffons, The 139
Chocolate Watchband 207
Chong, Tommy 181
Chords, The 11,32
CHUM Radio 132,134
Cimmoli, Bruno 54
CKDA Radio 54
CKLG Radio 150,161,164,165,175, 178,190,221
CKWX Radio 44,48,60,64,70,84,85, 86,94,221
Clanton, Jimmy 100
Clark, Dick 53,78,94,108,146,177

Clark, Petula 173
Clooney, Rosemary 8,9,23
Coasters, The 75
Cochran, Eddie 7,44,49,52,81,108
Cole, Natalie 118
Cole, Nat "King" 57,74,118
Collins, Dorothy 23
Collins, Judy 59,194
Columbia Records 48,75,177,199
Colony Club 100
Como, Perry 8,23,24,123
Cooke, Sam 7,48,126
Cookies, The 139
Cooley, Eddie 29
Coral Records 143
Country Joe and the Fish 207
Coupland, Knox 60
Cousteau, Jacques 122
Credence Clearwater Revival 210, 221
Crests, The 94
Crew Cuts 11,32
Crickets, The 156,173
Crosby, Bing 32,100
Crosby, David 178
Crosby, Gary 83
Crosby, Stills and Nash 178
Crystatte Records 94
Crystals, The (see also Curtis Lee) 127,139
Cullen, Jack 33,219
Curtola, Bobby 115,127,135

Daltry, Roger 207
Damone, Vic 23
Dana, Vic 100
Danny and the Juniors 75
Darren, Jimmy 108
Darin, Bobby 78,101,109,110,173 211
Dave Clark Five, The 161,168,172
David, Hal (see also Bacharach and David) 147,202
Davis, Jr., Sammy 9,182,221
Davis, Patti 118
Davis, Sheriff Tex (see Gene Vincent "Be Bop A Lulu") 87
Day, Doris 9,23
Dean, James 19,20,36,131
Dean, Jimmy 119
Dee, Joey and the Starlighters 126
Dees, Bill 169
DeShannon, Jackie 173
Detroit Wheels 199
Diamond, Neil 96,190,198,199
Diamonds, The 45,75
Diller, Phyllis 182,188,190,221
Dion 104,202
Diskin, Tom 60,65
Doc Records 86
Doe, Ernie K. 9
Doggett, Bill 29
Domino, Fats 28,29,49,130
Donegan, Lonnie 28
Donovan 186,194,195
Doors, The 169,197
Dorsey, Arnold George 207
Dorsey, Gerry 207
Dorsey, Tommy 22
Douglas, Kirk 84,135
Dragon, Carmen 118
Dragon, Daryl 118
Drifters, The 18,29,127,169
Dunaway, Faye 195
Dupres, Champion Jack 12
Duryea, Dan 108

Dylan, Bob 57,135,153,169,172, 178,187,194,221
Easybeats 198
Eddy, Duane 75,108
Elegant Parlor, The 181.182
Ellis, Shirley 173
Elphicke, Frank "Tiny" 85
Elvis Presley Music, Inc. 181
EMI Records 156
Emmons, Blake 189
Epstein, Brian (see also The Beatles) 156,160
Eric Burdon and the Animals 211
Esquires 198
Everly Brothers, The 44,45,49,75, 104,182
Evans, Ray 23
Fabian 104
Faithful and Marianne 217
Faith, Percy 109
Feld, Irvin 29
Feliciano, Jose 169
Fiedler, Arthur 178
Field, Elliott 86
Fifth Dimension 181,198,211,221
First Edition 211
Fisher, Eddie 24
Fitzgerald, Ella 28
Five Satins, The 29
Fleetwoods, The 100,104
Fogerty, Jim 210
Foley, Dick (see also Brothers Four) 100
Foley, Red 131
Fonda, Jane 217
Fonda, Peter 195
Fontana, D.J. 65
Fontane Sisters 11
Forst, Brian "Frosty" 143
Fountainbleau Hotel, Miami Beach 105
Four Lads, The 24,36
Four Tops, The 169,198
Franklin, Aretha 198,199
Francis, Connie 74,104,119,194
Frantics, The 100
Fraternity 109
Frato, Russ 29 (see also Chuck Berry and Allan Freed)
Freed, Allan 11,12,14,29,75,95,96
Freeman, Bobby 100
Friedan, Betty 217
Funicello, Annette 53

Gallant, Patsy 198
Garfunkel, Art 177
Garner, Erroll 52
Garner, James 23
Garnett, Gale 169
Gary U.S. Bonds 115
Gaye, Marvin 138,175
Gaynor, Mitzi 182,221
Gentry, Bobbie 115,182,183, 194,206
Georgia Hotel 60,182
Gerry and the Pacemakers 169
Getz, Stan 165,169
Gibson, Don 104,130
Gilberto, Astrid 165,169
Gilkyson, Terry 165
Ginn, Judy and Jim 221
Gladiolis, The 45
Gladys Knight and the Pips 199
Gleason, Jackie 24
Goffin, Gerry & Carol King 123,127
Goldsboro, Bobby 203,213
Gordy, Berry 138,182

Gore, Leslie 139
Goulet, Robert 198
Grant, Cary 23
Grass Roots 198
Gray, Glen 22
Greatful Dead, The 207
Greene, Lorne 22,169
Greenbert, Lawrence 147
Grimster, Ron 174
Guitar, Bonnie 74,87
Guthrie, Gary 96
Haley, Bill 6,7,9,11,12,14,15,19,
  20,28,32,33,36,45,84,114
Hamilton, George IV 49,57
Hamilton, Russ 57
Hampton, Lionel 29
Hancock, Hunter 11
Happenings, 198
Hatfield, Bobby 180,211
Hatch, Tony 173
Hardin, Glenn D. 142
Harper's Bazarre 211
Harris, Richard 203
Harris, Rolf 150,211,220
Harrison, George 139,197
Hawkins, Rompin' Ronnie 172,217
Hawn, Goldie 199
Hayes, Bruce 86
Hazelwood, Lee 190
Hell's Angels 216
Hendricks, Bobby 29
Hendrix, Jimi 216
Henn, Ernie 60
Hennessy, Roy 164,176,183
Henry, Gil 86
Heywood, Eddie 28
Hodgins, Peggy Keenan 67,134,
  146,150,164,165,182,190,219
Hoffman, Dustin 195
Holler, Dick 202
Holly, Buddy 6,7,15,19,44,49,52,
  86,115,142,153,156,172
Hollywood Argyles 109
Hopkins, Lightnin 14
Hopper, Dennis 195
Horton, Johnny 108
Hudson, Rock 23
Humperdinck, Engelbert 194,207
  (see also: Gerry Dorsey)
Hyland, Brian 109
Inkspots, The 29
Irish Rovers 206
Isley Brothers, The 126
Isy's Supper Club 181
Jacks, Terry 189
Jagger, Dean 83
Jagger, Mick 87,165,217
James, Harry 146
Janettes, The 139
Jardine, Al 176 (see also: Beach
  Boys)
Jarvis, Al 18,86
Jay, George 86
Jay and the Americans 198
Jefferson Airplane, The 210,216
Jennings, Waylon 49
John, Elton 118,207
Johnson, Arte 199
Jolson, Al 95,147,199
Jones, Brian 217
Jones, Carolyn 83
Jo, Damita 221
Jones, Tom 172,173,206,207
Jones, Jack 147
Joplin, Janis 194,210,216
Jordan, Al 143
Jordanaires, The 65,87

Jordan, Louis 13,14,29
Kaplan, Gabriel 179
Kallen, Kitty 9,146
Kelly, Grace 36
Kennedy, Jackie 114,153,213
Kennedy, John F. 104,110,
  111,114,153
Kennedy, Robert F. 202
Kenner, Chris 115
Kern, Gene 219
Kerouac, Jack 19
KFWB Radio 86
KGW Radio and Television 101,
  104,110
KHJ Radio 179
King, B.B. 13,28
"King Creole" (movie) 83
King, Ben E. 29
King, Claude 126
King, Martin Luther 202
King Records 12,18,29
KING Radio and Television 86
Kingsmen, The 151,173
Kingston Trio, The 33
Kitsilano Showboat, The 135
Kitt, Eartha 211
KNX 86
Knievel, Evel 119
Knox, Buddy 44,46,49,52,53
Kopelow, Ben 150
Kristofferson, Kris 194
Kubrick, Stanley 189
Laine, Frankie 8,9,24,49,150,
  182,210,211
Lancaster, Burt 135
LaPierre, Cherilyn 173
Larsen, Don 36
Latrimouille, Fred 188,189,190
Lawrence, Steve 101
Leary, Timothy 186
Led Zeppelin 216
Lee, Curtis 127
Lee, John M. 134
Lee, Peggy 23,86,87
Legrand, Michel 206
Legge, Peter 221
Lennon, John 159,160,164,
  181,186,187,199,202,217
Lewis, Jerry Lee 56,78,165
Lewis, Ramsay 165,181
Lewis, Shari 198,219
Liberty Records 115,143
Lightfoot, Gordon 135,146
Little Anthony and the Imperials
  96
Little Daddy and the Bachelors
  181
Little Eva 127
Little, Rich 135
Little Richard 28,56,87,130,134
Livingstone, Jay 23
London Coliseum 207
London School of Economics 165
Lopez, Trini 139,221
Lorenz, George "Hound Dog"
  11,18
Love, Mike (see also Beach
  Boys)176
Lowe, Jim 28
Luke, Robin 85
Luman, Bob 152
Lymon, Frankie 28,29,49,53,79
Mack, R. 139
Mamas and the Papas, The 186
Mancini, Henry 87,142

Mann, Barrie 177
Maple Leaf Ballroom 22
Magret, Ann 207
Martha and the Vandellas 138
Martin, Dean 87
Mason, Bonnie Jo 173
Mason, James 135
Mathis, Johnny 57,146
Matthau, Walter 83
Maugeri, Rudi 32
McCartney, Paul 160,178,
  186,199,202
McAdorey, Bob 134
McClure, Doug 108
McGuire Sisters 11,131,142
McGuire, Barry 187,195
McDaniels, Gene 115,122,123
McKuen, Rod 221
MacDonald, Jim 84
Maclean's 157
McLean, Don 115,152
McLendon, Gordon 56
McPhatter, Clyde 29
McRae, Sheila 221
Meader, Vaughan 153
Medley, Bill 180,211
Melson, Joe 115
Mercury Records 45,177,180,190
Mersey Sound 161
Metropolitan Opera House N.Y.C.
  207
Moonglows, The 12,142
Miller, Arthur 36
Miller, Chuck 57
Miller, Glenn 22
Miller, Mitch 24,75
Miller Roger 172
Millett, Kate 217
Mills, Gordon 206,207
Mineo, Sal 108
Mitchell, Guy 32,48
Moby Grape and The Heavenly
  Blues Band 207
Monkees 190,197,199
Monterey Pop Festival 194
Morgan, Robert W 179
Moore, Scotty 55
Moore, Terry 108
Monroe, Marilyn 36
Moss, Jerry 197
Motown Records 138,165,190
Murphy, Bridie 36
Murray, Anne 127,182,207
Murray, Arthur 127,180
Murray the K 178
Music Explosion 197
Muzak 186
Naylor, Jerry 142,156
Nelson, Rick 48,74,78,83,143
Nelson, Willie 44
Newhart, Bob 109
Newley, Anthony 221
Newman, Paul 220
Newport Folk Festival 172
Newton, Wayne 182
New Christy Minstrels 211
New Vaudeville Band 190,221
New York Times 134
Nite, Norman M. 86
Nitty Gritty Dirt Band 211
Nitzsche, Jack 195
Nixon, Vice-President Richard M.
  104,110
Nyro, Laura 181
Onassis, Aristotle 213
Ono, Yoko 202,217
Orbison, Roy 115,151,152,169,189

Orpheum Theatre 32,146,175
O'Sullivan, Gilbert 207
Otis, Johnnie 78
"Ozzie and Harriett" Show 48,78
Page, Billy 181
Page, Patti 8,9,23
Palmer, Dave 174
Parker, Col. Tom 48,56,60
  61,65,70,78,181
Parr, Jack 156
Parsons, Bill 109
Parsons, Tony 190
Parton, Dolly 44
Paul, Les and Mary Ford 9
Paul Revere and the Raiders 190
Peacock, Tom 143
Penguins, The 18
Perkins, Carl 15,28
Perkins, John 32
Perkins, Ray 32
Pesklevits, Susan 189
Peter, Paul & Mary 139,
  146,194,221
Phillips, Dewey 11,13
Phillips, John 186
Phillips, Mackenzie 186
Phillips, Michelle 186
Phillips Records 180
Phillips, Sam 56
Pickett, Hugh 60
Pitney, Gene 127
Platters, The 18,174
PNE 159
Porter, Don 110
Pomus 123
Prisonaires 36
Presley, Elvis 6,7,13,14
  15,19,20,26,28,32,33,36
  40,42,43,45,46,47,48,50
  51,52,54,56,58,60,61,64
  65,68,69,70,72,75,78,83
  84,87,94,97,102,104,105
  111,114,115,123,126,130
  131,146,156,170,172,181
  183,189,194,206,210,218
  220
Presley, Priscilla 61
Price, Alan 169
Price, Lloyd 96
Prima, Louis 87,221
Prince Charles 114
Pringle, Norm 86,87
Quant, Mary 187
Quantas Airlines 220
Quarrymen, The 153
Quicksilver Messenger Service
  207
Quillan, Tom 86
RCA 19,23,33,36
  56,60,65,109,152,219
Raines, Mark 61
Ram, Buck 18
Randall, Tony 23
Randle, Bill 32
Ray, Johnny 36,100
Rawls, Lou 122
RCA Records 180
Reagan, Ronald President 187
Reed, B. Mitchell 86
Reed, Oliver 207
Reeves, Jim 123
Rebel Rousers, The 108
Redding, Otis 194
Reisdorf, Bob 100
Reynolds, Debbie 45
Rhodes, Todd 12
Rich, Charlie 123,179,180,218

Richardson, J.P. (also known as The Big Bopper) 49,86
Richard, Cliff 146,152,218
Richards, J.J. 190
Riddel, Sam 179
Rigby, Eleanor 202
Righteous Brothers 180,182, 211,213,221
Rivera, Chita 182
Rivers, Johnny 181,182
Robbins, Marty 48,101,210
Robinson, Red 6,7,11,95, 157,159,160
Robinson, Smokey 138
Rock Around The Clock (song and movie) 9,13
Rodgers, Jimmy 57,211
Rogers, Kenny 211
Rolling Stones, The 14,18,29,161 164,165,169,198,212,216,217 220
Ronettes, The 139
Rooftop Singers 139
Rooney, Mickey 108
Rose, David 126
Rowan and Martin 199
Ross, Katherine 195
Ross, Diana and the Supremes 7,104 138,165,173,182,188,190,194
Royal Gardsman, The 197
Russell, Bobby 203
Rusty & Doug 14
Rydell, Bobby 108,153
Ryder, Mitch 199
Sager Carol Bayer 147
Sam the Sham and the Pharoahs 172
Sands, Tommy 48,83
Sandpipers, The 221
Satie, Eric 220
Scott, Jack 109
Seals and Croft 75
Sebastian, John 178
Sedaka, Neil 118,126
Sedaka, Dara 118
Seekers, The 172,197
Seven Up 22
Seeger, Pete 57,139,142,178,194
Shannon, Del 115,156
Sherman, Allan 150
Shields, Brooke 207
Shultz, Charles 197
Shuman, 123
Sugal, Don 105
Silhouettes, The 75
Silverstein, Shel 206
Simon and Garfunkel 177,187, 195,206,211,213
Sinatra, Frank 21,24,36,48 53,104,105,110,123,152 172,186,190,194,206
Sinatra, Nancy 190
Simpson, Russ 164,165
Slaight, Allan 134
Slick, Grace 210
Sly and the Family Stone 216,220
Smith, Keely 87
Sonny and Cher 173,176,198,221
Soul Survivors 197
South, Joe 210
Spencer, Lady Diana 114
St. Marie, Buffy 180,195
Stafford, Jo 23
Stafford, Kay 8,9
Starr, Ringo (see The Beatles) 157,160

Stauffer, Ken 182,183
Steinem, Gloria 217
Stewart, Jimmy 135
Stevens, Dodie 94
Stoller, Mike 75
Stone, Jesse 29
Strawberry Alarm Clock 197
Streisand, Barbra 96,139, 169,173,206
Stray Cats 222
Storm, Gale 87
Storz, Todd 56
Sullivan, Ed 44,156
Sun Label 19,28,36,56,179
Supremes 198
Susanne, Jacqueline 189
Suzuki, Pat 100,211
Tanner, "Jolly" John 168,176
Taylor, Bobby and the Vancouvers 182
Teen Canteen 44,65
Temptations 198
Tenille, Toni 118
"They Shoot Horses Don't They?" (movie) 119
Thomas, David Clayton 220
Thomas, B.J. 189,220
Three Dog Night 33
Tillotson, Johnny 109
"Time is on my Side" 164
Tom and Jerry 177
Tommy Scott and The Senators 206
Townshend, Peter 207
Travolta, John 179
Trudeau, Pierre Elliott 114
Trudeau, Margaret 217
Trudeau, Prime Minister P.E. 217
Turner, Ike 118
Turner, Joe 11
Turner, Tina 118,119
Twitty, Conway (Also known as Harold Jenkins) 75,108
Tyson, Ian (see The Stripes) 151
Union Gap, The 199
U.S. Congress 94
Valens, Ritchie 7,49,86
Valient 109
Vancouver Media Club 219
Vancouver Sun, The 83,95,160
Van Doren, Mamie 108
Vaughan, Sarah 28
Vee, Bobby 115
Ventures, The 100,108
Vincent, Gene 7,28,74,87,108,131
Vinton, Bobby 115,169
Volchuck, Zollie 60
Vogt, Les 143
WJW 11,12
Warwick, Dionne 147,198,221
Wasserman, Jack 83,160
Waters, Vic 219
Weavers, The 57
Webb, Jimmy 180,181,203,219
Weill, Cynthia 176
Weld, Tuesday 108
Will Mastin Trio 221
WINS Radio 12
West Side Story (play & movie) 119
Whiskey A-Go-Go 181
WHO 207,216
Williams, Andy 49,123,142
Williams, Hank 12,36
Williams, Paul 198
Williams, Tony 18
Williams, Roger 24

Willis, Chuck 78
Wilson, Brian 138,180
Wilson, Nancy 186
Winterhalter, Hugo 28
Wonder, Stevie 138,190
Woodstock 178,216
Woolley, Sheb 75
Yocam, Joe 86
Young, Bruce 95
Young, Rascals 197
Zombies, The 169